*The
Connell Guide
to*

The Tudors

by Susan Doran

Contents

Introduction: Who were the Tudors?   6

Dynastic Right and Royal Succession
How serious were the dynastic challenge?   11
Why did the succession become a problem for Henry VIII?   18
How did Henry VIII try to secure the succession after his annulment?   24
Why was there a succession crisis in 1553?   28
How serious was the Catholic challenge to Elizabeth?   30
How did Elizabeth deal with the succession?   34

Religious Reformations
How strong was the English Church before the break with Rome?   40
Why did Henry VIII introduce religious change?   46
Why were there so many changes in religion between 1547 and 1559?   51
How did parishioners react to religious change?   56
Why were Protestants critical of the Elizabethan Church?   64
How dangerous were the Puritans?   68

Government, politics and protest
Did the Tudors introduce innovations in Government?   72
Did parliament become more important?   76

How important was factional in-fighting?	80
Was there a Tudor despotism?	86
Why were there so many rebellions in England?	90
How did the Tudors deal with Ireland?	98

Foreign relations
How did England's relations with France change?	103
Why did England go to war against Spain in 1585?	111

Conclusion 116

NOTES

Chronology of the Tudor Dynasty	*13*
Bonds, Recognizances and Attainders	*14*
Cardinal Thomas Wolsey	*22*
Anne Boleyn's relationship with Henry	*24*
Mary Queen of Scots	*33*
England under the Tudors	*36*
Who believed what?	*42*
The process of Henry VIII's Reformation	*46*
The Edwardian Reformation	*52*
Confessional divisions	*55*
Ten Facts about the Tudors	*60*
Penal laws against Catholics	*64*
Who were the Puritans?	*68*
Mid-Tudor risings	*92*
Glossary and Who's Who	*119*
Further reading	*122*

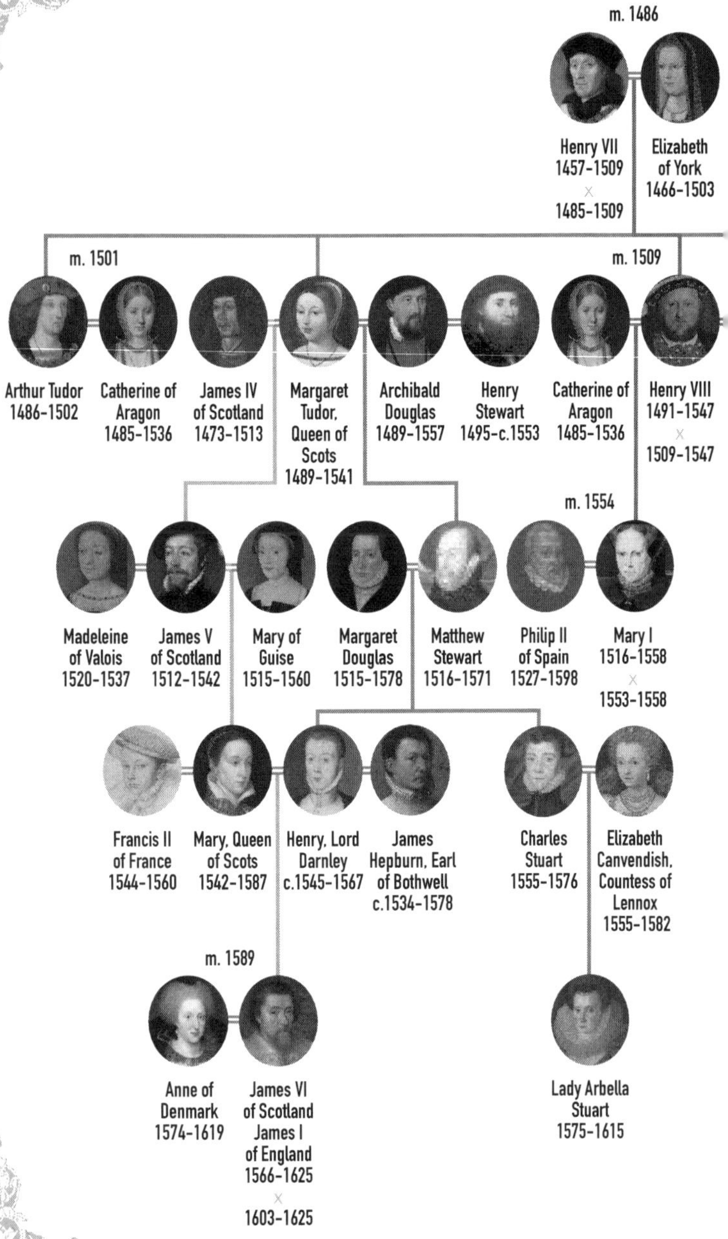

m. 1486

Henry VII
1457-1509
×
1485-1509

Elizabeth
of York
1466-1503

m. 1501

m. 1509

Arthur Tudor
1486-1502

Catherine of
Aragon
1485-1536

James IV
of Scotland
1473-1513

Margaret
Tudor, Queen
of Scots
1489-1541

Archibald
Douglas
1489-1557

Henry
Stewart
1495-c.1553

Catherine of
Aragon
1485-1536

Henry VIII
1491-1547
×
1509-1547

m. 1554

Madeleine
of Valois
1520-1537

James V
of Scotland
1512-1542

Mary of
Guise
1515-1560

Margaret
Douglas
1515-1578

Matthew
Stewart
1516-1571

Philip II
of Spain
1527-1598

Mary I
1516-1558
×
1553-1558

Francis II
of France
1544-1560

Mary, Queen
of Scots
1542-1587

Henry, Lord
Darnley
c.1545-1567

James
Hepburn, Earl
of Bothwell
c.1534-1578

Charles
Stuart
1555-1576

Elizabeth
Canvendish,
Countess of
Lennox
1555-1582

m. 1589

Anne of
Denmark
1574-1619

James VI
of Scotland
James I
of England
1566-1625
×
1603-1625

Lady Arbella
Stuart
1575-1615

HOUSE OF TUDOR
1485–1603
FAMILY TREE

m. (2) 1533	m. (3) 1536	m. (4) 1540	m. (5) 1540	m. (6) 1543			
						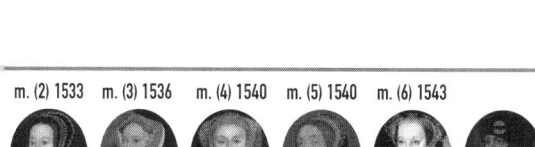	
Anne Boleyn c.1501–1536	Jane Seymour c.1508–1537	Anne of Cleves 1515–1557	Katherine Howard c.1518–1542	Catherine Parr 1512–1548	Louis XII of France 1462–1515	Mary Tudor, Queen of France 1496–1533	Charles Brandon, Duke of Suffolk c.1484–1545

Elizabeth I
1533–1603
1558–1603

Edward IV
1537–1553
1547–1553

Henry Grey, Duke of Suffolk 1517–1554

Frances Brandon 1517–1559

Guildford Dudley c.1535–1554 | Lady Jane Grey 1537–1554 | Lady Katherine Grey c.1540–1568 | Lady Mary Grey c.1546–1578

Introduction: Who were the Tudors?

Henry VII (1485-1509)

August 22nd 1485 is one of the most important dates in the history of the British monarchy. It is the day Henry VII, as he became, won the Battle of Bosworth Field and took the throne. The crown has remained in the line of his heirs ever since.

Tall with striking blue eyes, Henry was the only child of Edmund Tudor, Earl of Richmond, and Margaret Beaufort. His paternal grandparents were Owen Tudor, a Welsh squire, and Queen Katherine, the French-born widow of Henry V. On his mother's side, he was descended from the bastard line of John of Gaunt, Duke of Lancaster. Henry therefore saw himself as a Lancastrian.

In 1571, at the age of 14, he had escaped from England to France during the Wars of the Roses. As the main Lancastrian claimant to the throne, his life was in danger after the Yorkist Edward IV had seized the throne for a second time. Returning to England in 1485, he defeated Richard III at Bosworth. (Richard had himself usurped the throne in 1483 on his brother Edward IV's death.)

Crowned Henry VII at the age of 28, the first Tudor King fought off pretenders for much of his reign. Once king, he married the Yorkist princess, Elizabeth, a union that brought together the warring houses of Lancaster (the red rose) and York (the white rose). Their children were on both sides descended from Edward III and thought of as Plantagenets. The Tudor surname was never used in official publications, and hardly at all in writings before 1584. Only in later histories has the dynasty become known as the Tudors.

Henry VIII (1509-47)

He was nearly 18 when he inherited the throne. Very tall (6ft 2ins), athletic, a fluent Latin and French speaker and a talented musician, he has been described as "a Renaissance prince to his fingertips". But he was ruthless and constantly sought scapegoats. His contemporary, the Italian Machiavelli (though he never met Henry), described him as "rich, ferocious and greedy for glory"; others compared him to the Roman emperors Nero and Tiberius. On his deathbed, Henry VII had advised his son to marry his brother Arthur's widow, the graceful and pious 23-year-old **Katherine of Aragon**. Henry was captivated by her when they married but they grew apart as she aged. All but one of the six children Katherine conceived were stillborn, miscarried or died shortly after childbirth.

By 1527 Henry had fallen for **Anne Boleyn**. His determination to marry her resulted in the break with Rome, as the Pope refused to annul the King's marriage to Katherine. Henry secretly wed Anne in

1533, but three years later she was executed, after failing to give him a son. Unlike Anne, his third wife, **Jane Seymour**, stayed out of politics, choosing the motto: "Bound to obey and serve." She died soon after giving birth to a son, Edward.

Then came two short-lived marriages, the first to the German **Anne of Cleves** and the second to **Katherine Howard**, who was hardly more than a teenager when Henry married her, and who was then caught in an adulterous relationship and executed. The King wept and complained of his "ill luck in meeting with such ill-conditioned wives". Finally, he wed the 30-year-old **Katherine Parr**, twice widowed, lively, attractive and clever. By now, Henry was troubled by an ulcerous leg and very fat. In his last few years, he was pushed around his chambers in special (wheel)chairs called "trams".

Edward VI (1547-53)

Only nine years old when his reign began, he was arguably England's best-educated king. Like his father, he was highly intelligent and enjoyed music, jousts and entertainments. He was also a zealous Protestant and his last words were said to be: "Oh my lord God, defend this realm from papistry." Though short, his reign was notable for introducing Protestantism to England.

Lady Jane Grey (10-19 July, 1553)

Fifteen when proclaimed Queen, she ruled for just nine days. "The crown is not my right... and pleaseth me not. The Lady Mary is the rightful heir," she said when she became Queen.

After months of imprisonment in the Tower of London, she was executed, aged 16.

Mary (1553-58)

Apart from Lady Jane Grey, she was England's first female ruler.

As a young princess, she received a sound Classical education and showed herself accomplished in music and other skills. When her father married Anne Boleyn, she was declared a bastard and for a time excluded from court. As a devout Catholic, she refused to stop celebrating Mass in her own household during Edward's reign.

Once Queen, she married Philip, then Prince and later King of Spain, but they had no children. Her reign is best remembered for the burning of Protestants and the loss of Calais, England's last territory in France.

Elizabeth (1558-1603)

When Elizabeth was born on 7 September, 1533, it

was a great disappointment to her father, Henry VIII, and a catastrophe for her mother, Anne Boleyn. Astrologers, doctors and midwives had all assured them that their first child would be a boy.

After her mother's execution, Elizabeth – like her half-sister – was declared a bastard. Brought up a Protestant, she was treated as an object of suspicion under Mary. Aged 20, she was taken as a prisoner to the Tower of London for two months, and then transferred to Woodstock, with 60 soldiers standing guard. She etched on her window pane with a diamond: "Much suspected of me, nothing proved can be. Quoth Elizabeth, prisoner."

In the first 18 months of her reign, Elizabeth's intimacy with Robert Dudley was a source of salacious gossip: Dudley was already married and in 1560 his wife was found dead at the foot of a small stone staircase. It has never been established whether or not this was an accident. Elizabeth decided marrying him was too dangerous but remained very close to him even after his second marriage in 1578. Despite the gossip, there is no evidence Elizabeth had a sexual relationship with him or anyone else.

She never met her Scottish cousin, Mary Stewart (Queen of Scots), yet their relationship dominated English politics from 1558 to Mary's execution in early 1587. Robert Cecil, Elizabeth's adviser throughout her reign, worried constantly about the "SQ", as he referred to her. It is said he couldn't bear to speak her name. While the defeat of the Spanish

Armada in 1588 was Elizabeth's greatest triumph, the execution of Mary (which she never meant to authorise) affected her far more deeply.

Elizabeth presided over a golden age of English letters, with Shakespeare writing many of his greatest plays during her reign.

Dynastic Right and Royal Succession

How serious were dynastic challenges to the early Tudors?

All the Tudor monarchs were beset by two problems: did they have a right to the throne? And who should succeed them? The question of legitimacy was there from the start – with Henry VII's dubious claim to the throne.

Henry was the last man standing as a potential Lancastrian king, but males from the Yorkist line – especially the four nephews of Edward IV – had a far stronger hereditary right. Consequently, Henry claimed the throne not just by bloodline but (as he saw it) by God's judgment on the field of battle, even though he dated his reign from the day *before* Bosworth. He also ensured that his title was buttressed by a 1485 parliamentary statute and a 1486 papal bull. His marriage to the 19-year-old Elizabeth of York, the eldest daughter of Edward IV, won over many doubters among the nobility and was praised for uniting the houses of Lancaster and York. Nonetheless, Henry had to face dangerous dynastic challenges.

The first of these came from Lambert Simnel. Simnel was a ten-year-old commoner groomed by a priest with Yorkist sympathies to impersonate Edward IV's nephew, Edward, Earl of Warwick, then a prisoner in the Tower of London. In need of a figurehead, Yorkist loyalists took Lambert over to Ireland, where he was crowned King Edward VI. The loyalists then landed in England with mercenary troops and an Irish army, hoping to raise the North against Henry. But the support they attracted was disappointing. Henry's strategy of treating Richard III's followers leniently after Bosworth served him well: most nobles stayed loyal. Besides, doubts existed about Simnel's legitimacy, especially once Henry had paraded the real Warwick through the streets of London.

As it marched south, the rebel force of about 8,000 met Henry's larger army and was decisively defeated at Stoke on 16 June 1487. This battle was effectively the final military engagement of the Wars of the Roses. Most men in the Yorkist army were slaughtered, but Simnel was captured and sent to work in the royal kitchens.

Nearly five years later, Henry faced another imposter. A Flemish youth, Perkin Warbeck, professed to be Richard, Duke of York, the younger of the two missing "Princes in the Tower"*, the sons of Edward IV. Until Warbeck's capture and confession in September 1497, virtually no one could be certain that he was *not* the Yorkist King's heir. So he garnered support, at different times, from continental courts, the King of Scotland, powerful lords in Ireland, members of Henry's own household, and even Cornish rebels who were protesting about royal taxes in 1497.

Henry responded to the Warbeck crises in a

* See glossary on page 114 for phrases and names coloured in the text.

CHRONOLOGY OF THE TUDOR DYNASTY

1485 The Battle of Bosworth; Henry VII's coronation (30 Oct).
1586 Henry's marriage to Elizabeth of York (18 Jan); Prince Arthur's birth (Sep).
1491 Prince Henry's birth (28 Jun).
1501 Arthur's marriage to Katherine of Aragon (14 Nov).
1502 Arthur's death (Apr).
1503 Elizabeth of York's death (Feb).
1509 Henry VII dies (21 Apr); Henry VIII marries Katherine of Aragon (Jun).
1516 Princess Mary born (Feb).
1533 Henry VIII marries Anne Boleyn. Princess Elizabeth born (Sep).
1536 Anne executed (May).
1537 Prince Edward born (Oct).
1544 Henry VIII's third Succession Act, restoring Mary and Elizabeth to the royal succession.
1547 Edward VI comes to the throne (28 Jan).
1553 Edward dies (6 Jul). Succession crisis. Mary crowned.
1558 Elizabeth comes to the throne (17 Nov).
1603 Elizabeth dies (Mar). ∎

range of ways. To counter foreign aid for the pretender, he threatened punitive expeditions and afterwards reached agreements with rulers abroad. At home, he used bonds and recognizances to keep the loyalty of his nobility and important gentry; when men looked disloyal, they suffered arrests, executions and attainders. To foster support for his dynasty, Henry arranged magnificent celebrations around royal events: Arthur's elevation as Prince of Wales in November 1489; his brother Henry's installation as Knight of the Bath and Duke of York

BONDS, RECOGNIZANCES AND ATTAINDERS

The bond was a contractual agreement of good behaviour between an individual and the monarch.

The recognizance, created as part of the legal process, was used to enforce a bond. It usually included agreements to abide by certain conditions, such as payments of a fine, appearance before the council or court at a future date, or restrictions on movements.

Attainders were statutory acts of parliament that imposed penalties for high treason without the need for judicial proceedings. The king could pardon the capital sentence and restore the forfeiture of lands if he chose.

Henry VII used bonds, recognizances and attainders to tie his great men into a set of obligations which had penalty clauses. This was not a new device but he used it more widely, intensively and systematically than had earlier monarchs to keep nobles loyal.

Between 1437 and 1458, 22 peers had been under bonds and recognizances at one time or another but under Henry VII 36 out of 62 senior noble families were under bonds and recognizances, while 23 other in October 1494; and Arthur's proxy betrothal ceremony to the Spanish princess Katherine of Aragon in August 1497.

Eventually, in 1498, Warbeck was imprisoned in the Tower. A year later, he was implicated in a plot to set free Warwick, his fellow-prisoner, and place him on the throne. Both men were beheaded in November 1499. Before his execution, Warbeck was forced to make another public declaration that he was no Plantagenet.

Even after this, Henry did not feel secure. Three leading families were under bonds more than once during the reign. The number of bonds Henry imposed accelerated after 1502, when he became worried about the succession.

Another seven noblemen, as well as numerous gentlemen, were tied to him by attainder. Henry revoked the capital sentence in these cases and allowed a probationary period during which the nobleman's forfeited lands might be restored if the penitent "traitor" proved loyal.

Historians have long debated whether Henry's methods were overly harsh. Among the strongest critics are Christine Carpenter and John Guy, who say he massively alienated the nobility. Steven Gunn, however, offers a more nuanced assessment. He accepts that a "slide towards tyranny" was a characteristic of Henry's rule but maintains that the King's rigour was in the interests of "good governance". Henry's fiscal initiatives and procedures to ensure that the most powerful men in the localities were loyal "made his government of England and that of his successors more ambitious and more powerful than any that had gone before". ■

* Henry VII: Founder of Stability or Incompetent Monarch? The Tudors www.tudors.org › AS/A2 Level (Accessed 2016); Steven Gunn, *Henry VII's New Men and the Making of Tudor England* (Oxford, 2016).

royal deaths within three years – those of his youngest son Edmund, his first-born Arthur, and his wife Elizabeth – meant that the future of his dynasty after 1503 rested on the life of his second son, Prince Henry. The de la Pole brothers, nephews of the two Yorkist Kings, were his greatest concern, although in reality the pair – Edmund, Earl of Suffolk, and Richard de la Pole – could muster little support in England or abroad. Edmund, moreover, was captured in 1506 and imprisoned in the Tower.

But Henry, now in poor health, still feared that there would be plots against him and his under-age heir if he did not keep his nobility under close supervision and control. The increased use of bonds and recognizances during his last years may well have been due to this troubling concern and not – as the contemporary chronicler Polydore Vergil alleged – to Henry's greedy desire to boost the crown's finances. Vergil accused Henry of avarice, a vice which distorted "those qualities of trustfulness, justice and integrity by which the state must be governed".

Henry's worries, though, were overblown. His son's accession in April 1509 was undisputed. Indeed, the new King was the first to succeed to the English throne peaceably for more than 85 years. Nonetheless, the transfer of power was accompanied by what Steven Gunn has called a "partisan political manoeuvre" amounting to "a coup".[*]

---

[*] S. J. Gunn, 'The Accession of Henry VIII', *Historical Research*, 64 (1991), pp.278-88

*The Whitehall Mural by Remigius van Leemput.
Clockwise from left: Henry VIII, Henry VII, Elizabeth of York and Jane Seymour*

Henry VII's death was kept secret for 48 hours so that an aristocratic group of councillors and courtiers could oust from power Sir Richard Empson and Edmund Dudley, the old king's unpopular advisers and financial agents.

During the early years of the new reign the young Henry VIII won the support of his great men by cancelling the recognizances imposed on them and issuing a general pardon for past offences. Supported by his nobility, Henry VIII had no cause to fear a domestic challenge to his throne. In June 1512, however, when he went to war against France, Louis XII recognised the Yorkist Richard de la Pole as England's king. In reaction Henry ordered the execution of de la Pole's older brother, Edmund, before he journeyed to the Continent with his army. The Anglo-French treaty of peace in 1514 isolated Richard, who was killed in the 1525 Battle of Pavia.

Not until his break with Rome did Henry fear another challenge to the crown. But when his cousin, Cardinal Reginald Pole, encouraged the Pope to issue a bull excommunicating and deposing him, Henry – out of fear and revenge – had most of the surviving Yorkists arrested and imprisoned, including the Cardinal's brother (Henry, Lord Montagu), mother (Margaret, Countess of Salisbury) and cousin (Henry Courtenay, Marquess of Exeter), all three of whom were later executed. The beheading of the 67 year-old Margaret in May 1541 was particularly brutal not only because of her age but also because Henry did not employ a professional executioner. He left her, instead, in the hands of an inexperienced youth "who literally hacked her head and shoulders to pieces in the most pitiful manner" (as the Spanish ambassador reported). Margaret's fate was widely criticised at the time, and in 1886 she was beatified as a martyr of the Catholic Church.

Why did the succession become a problem for Henry VIII?

The succession caused Henry VIII a greater problem than it had his father and much personal heartache. His first wife Katherine of Aragon (Arthur's widow) conceived at least six times but only two children were born alive. On New Year's Day 1511, she delivered a boy who survived just two months. In 1516 she gave birth to Mary, a grave disappointment for Henry who was desperate for a son. In 1519 Katherine became pregnant for the last time, but again unsuccessfully.

With a girl as his only direct heir, Henry worried that a usurper might seize the throne on his death. His anxiety on this score explains the execution of Edward Stafford, Duke of Buckingham, another descendant of Edward III, in 1521. Told that Buckingham was listening to prophesies that he might one day be king, Henry had him put on trial for treason. This judicial murder of an important nobleman was a foretaste of Henry's later acts of paranoia and tyranny.

Initially, Henry held Katherine responsible for the lack of a male heir. After all, his mistress Elizabeth Blount gave birth to a son so the fault, he thought, could not be his. In the same year as his illegitimate son was born – 1519 – he brought doctors over from Spain to examine his 34-year-old wife, but to no avail. By the mid 1520s, he had lost hope that Katherine would conceive again.

What was he to do? According to some contemporary reports, he considered making his bastard son, named Henry Fitzroy, his heir. Certainly, once the child had survived the dangers of infant mortality, the King bestowed unusual favour upon him. Not since the reign of Henry II had a royal bastard been raised to the peerage, yet in 1525 Henry gave the six-year-old the titles of Earl of Nottingham, Duke of Richmond (Henry VII's pre-Bosworth title) and Duke of Somerset (the title held by Henry's late brother, Edmund). The boy was now the senior nobleman in England; unsurprisingly, Katherine was said to be "dissatisfied" with his elevation. Possibly for this reason Henry sent their nine-year-old daughter, Mary, to Ludlow Castle in the style of previous princes of Wales, a move that signalled her status as heir presumptive.

Two years later, Henry found another solution to the succession problem. In May 1527, he publicly questioned the validity of his marriage to Katherine on the grounds that their failure to produce a son was God's punishment for an unlawful union. In marrying Arthur's widow, declared Henry, he had disobeyed the scriptural prohibition against taking to bed a brother's wife. The relevant verses in Leviticus (18:16 and 20:21) warned this sin would be punished by childlessness, a term which – according to one Hebrew scholar – meant "son-less". At the time of their wedding in 1503, the Pope had issued a dispensation to remove the impediment of affinity (i.e. being in a close relationship), but Henry now argued that no dispensation could waive God's law as propounded in the scriptures.

Had the King appealed to technical flaws in the original document, as he was advised to do, he might have been more successful. Instead, convinced his marriage was sinful in the eyes of God, he unrealistically expected Pope Clement VII to admit that papal powers were limited, and to do so at a time when Martin Luther was already challenging papal supremacy in Germany. Had he decided to marry a French princess, rather than the commoner Anne Boleyn, he might have mustered more support. As it was, most people believed that Henry was motivated more by lust than reasons of state in his search for an annulment. The humanist scholar Desiderius Erasmus suggested he "should take two Junos rather than put away one", and even the Pope recommended a bigamous arrangement.

The international situation also worked against Henry. Katherine had a powerful ally in her nephew Charles, the Holy Roman Emperor and King of Spain, who dominated the Italian peninsula. In May 1527 Imperialist troops sacked Rome and held the Pope prisoner. Only a resurgence of French power in Italy would give the Pope the freedom to offend Charles and grant an annulment, but the French King, Francis I, proved unable to oust the Imperialists from Northern Italy. Indeed, a French army was decisively beaten at Landriano, a defeat that resulted in Pope Clement signing a peace treaty with Charles on 29 June 1529.

As a result of these difficulties, Cardinal Wolsey spent two years unsuccessfully pressing the Pope to let him judge the annulment case in England without recourse to Rome. And when Clement eventually permitted a legatine court (a court presided over by Wolsey as papal legate) to be held at Blackfriars in London during June 1529, the proceedings proved disastrous for the King. Katherine formally appealed to Rome and publicly swore that she had never slept with Arthur so that her marriage to Henry was valid. The next month, Clement revoked the case and took it to the papal court in Rome. With the Pope the ally of the Emperor, Henry had little chance of obtaining an annulment. In October, Wolsey fell from power and the King began an attack on the Church.

CARDINAL THOMAS WOLSEY

Born the son of an Ipswich butcher and educated at Oxford, Wolsey entered royal service as Henry VII's chaplain. Just before and during Henry VIII's French campaign of 1512 he established himself at court, taking charge of preparing supplies for the army. Wolsey's remarkable energy and organisational skills ensured further promotions in Church and state. Over the next two decades, he took over the routine tasks of managing the kingdom, acted as Lord Chancellor (appointed 1515), and devoted himself to international diplomacy. Wolsey became Henry's confidant and most influential counsellor, though not an independent policy maker. Wolsey was simply the King's servant, dedicated to advancing the royal will.

Wolsey was the most powerful cleric in England, known to foreign ambassadors as the "second king" or *alter rex*. Diplomats also christened him "the second pope", or *alter papa*. He held many rich bishoprics (including the Archbishopric of York), was made cardinal in 1515, and became *legate a latere* (the highest form of papal legate) in

After Wolsey's fall, Henry worked on presenting his case to Rome, seeking a ruling in his favour from the most prestigious universities in Europe. Some time in 1530, however, he changed tack and began questioning a pope's right ever to hear English cases in Rome. Questioning papal jurisdiction in England led him down the road towards the royal supremacy. Over the next couple of years, he decided to sever links with Rome and take command of the Church himself. In May 1533 he eventually secured his annulment – not from the

1518, which meant that he outranked the Archbishop of Canterbury.

Wolsey's failure to obtain the annulment angered both Henry and Anne. In October 1529, he was indicted on a charge of *praemunire* (the criminal offence of asserting papal jurisdiction in England, and so restricting the power of the English monarch) and deprived of the lord chancellorship. Was he the victim of faction? Yes, according to David Starkey and Eric Ives, who detected Anne and rival noblemen conspiring against him. No, according to Peter Gwyn and George Bernard, who argue that Henry "really did not require a faction to tell him … that Wolsey's divorce plans were not succeeding".[*]

Granted a full pardon in February 1530, Wolsey left London for his Archdiocese of York. The following October, he was accused of treason. Whether this charge was true or fabricated by his enemies is again disputed by historians. Wolsey died on route to London where he would have been executed. ■

[*] David Starkey, *The Reign of Henry VIII. Personalities and Politics* (London, 1985); E. Ives, 'The Fall of Wolsey', in Steven J Gunn, Phillip G. Lindley (eds), *Cardinal Wolsey: Church, State and Art* (Cambridge, 1991), pp. 186-315; Peter Gwyn, *The King's Cardinal: The Rise and Fall of Thomas Wolsey* (London, 1990); G. W. Bernard, 'The Fall of Wolsey Reconsidered', *Journal of British Studies*, 35 (1996), 277-310.

Pope, but from Thomas Cranmer, the new Archbishop of Canterbury. By then Henry had already secretly married Anne.

How did Henry VIII try to secure the succession after his annulment?

In September 1533, Anne delivered a daughter, Elizabeth, whom most people thought was a bastard. Not only had she been conceived before her parents' marriage in January 1533, but she was born during Katherine's lifetime. Though frustrated by her sex,

ANNE BOLEYN'S RELATIONSHIP WITH HENRY

According to Eric Ives, Henry was already considering an annulment in 1526 when Anne caught his fancy, and her refusal to become his mistress propelled him to act. More controversially, George Bernard believes that Henry decided to make Anne his wife *after* they were lovers and then ended their sexual relationship so that any child conceived would be legitimate.*

Ives and Bernard also disagree about Anne's influence on political life. Ives thinks she played a role in Wolsey's fall. Bernard is unconvinced, and disputes the portrayal of Anne as a promoter of religious reform. As for Anne's fall, Ives thinks Anne was the victim of a court conspiracy, engineered by Thomas Cromwell, whereas Bernard thinks she was probably guilty of adultery with at least one of the five men accused. On both counts, Ives's account is the more convincing. ∎

* Eric W. Ives, *Anne Boleyn* (Oxford, 1986); G. W Bernard, *Anne Boleyn: Fatal Attractions* (New Haven, 2010).

Anne Boleyn (c.1501 - 1536)

Henry was determined that she and not Mary would be accepted as his heir until a boy was born, so the baby Elizabeth was called "Princess", whereas her elder sister was demoted to the "Lady Mary". To establish in law Elizabeth's hereditary right to the throne, and that of any future sons, Henry introduced a parliamentary bill in 1534 which declared the invalidity of his union with Katherine, the legality of his second marriage, and the legitimacy of his issue with Anne.

But no son was born. After two miscarriages, Anne became vulnerable and disposable. In May 1536 she was accused of multiple adulteries, incest and high treason. (The alleged adultery was with members of the King's privy chamber and the incest with her brother, George. Anne and George were both beheaded after their trial, at which no witnesses were called against them.) Two days before her execution, Cranmer declared her marriage to Henry invalid, a verdict making nonsense of the accusations of adultery. That same summer parliament passed a second Succession Act, pronouncing the marriage's invalidity and hence Elizabeth's bastardy. Furthermore, this statute asserted the revolutionary principle that Henry had full power to assign the crown to a successor of his choice, if he had no legitimate heirs of his body.

The birth of Edward in 1537, however, gave Henry an indisputable heir. Both his ex-wives were dead when the boy was born to Queen Jane (Seymour). But Jane died from complications following childbirth, and after two further marriages – an unconsummated union with Anne of Cleves, annulled in 1540, and a marriage to Katherine Howard which ended in her execution in 1542 – Henry still had only one legal heir. In 1543, he married Katherine Parr and hoped for another son. In the meantime, he decided to make further arrangements for the succession.

In 1544 another Succession Act was passed by Parliament. Contravening common law, which excluded bastards from inheritance, Henry brought his daughters back into the succession without legitimating them. He also reaffirmed the principle that he could lay down the future line of succession in a document "signed with his most gracious hand".

This he did in his last will of December 1547, when he confirmed his bastard daughters' place in the succession and made further provision if all his children died without issue.

Ignoring the better hereditary claim of the Stewart progeny of his elder sister Margaret, Henry stipulated that the succession should fall to the descendants of his younger sister Mary (the Suffolk line) but skip over his niece Frances. The omission of the Stewarts was understandable, given Henry's determination that Mary, the young Queen of Scotland, should marry his son Edward; bypassing Frances in favour of his sister's female offspring was done in the hope that she or her daughters would later produce a male heir.

Despite the new succession act, Henry continued to fret that his son might be deposed because of his youth. Now a sick man, he became increasingly paranoid and, in December 1546, brought to trial and had executed the soldier and poet Henry Howard, Earl of Surrey, when the nobleman displayed the royal arms and those of Edward the Confessor on his escutcheon (the emblem bearing a coat of arms). Surrey's father, Thomas, third Duke of Norfolk, was attainted at the same time but spared execution by the death of the King; Norfolk remained in the Tower until Mary came to the throne.

Why was there a succession crisis in 1553 and how was it resolved?

On Edward VI's death in July 1553, a succession dispute occurred that could easily have led to civil war but ended surprisingly peacefully. The crisis arose because the young king had decided to overturn his father's 1544 statute and remove his half-sisters from the succession. Knowing Mary would reintroduce Catholicism and fearing Elizabeth might marry a Catholic, Edward's concern had been to protect his recent Protestant settlement. He justified his sisters' exclusion on the grounds that they were both bastards, unmarried women, and only in the half-blood.

Initially, Edward planned to bar *all* women from the throne. In his undated "Devise for the Succession", he excluded all the female Suffolk heirs named in Henry's will in favour of an as yet unborn male son of any one of them. Most historians believe that the King wrote this original "Devise" without consulting his chief councillor, John Dudley, Duke of Northumberland, but they disagree about its timing. When his health was failing, Edward amended the "Devise" in late May or early June 1553. He now bequeathed the crown to the unimpeachably Protestant Lady Jane Grey (the daughter of Frances, Duchess of Suffolk) who had married Northumberland's son, Guildford Dudley, on 21 May 1553.

Eric Ives concludes that Edward remained the

"driving force" behind this new "Devise", but Dale Hoak has compellingly argued that Edward was by this time being advised by the Duke of Northumberland and several Protestants in the privy chamber who were the Duke's allies. In mid June, the realm's leading judges – acting under duress – drew up letters patent authorising this succession on condition that parliament agreed to it.

Edward's scheme collapsed because of his premature death and Mary's determined actions. He died on 6 July before parliament could meet and legitimise Jane's succession. Mary – alerted by a friendly councillor to Edward's terminal illness – escaped capture by refusing to obey the privy council's summons to London, issued before the King's death. She slipped away from her manor at Hunsdon in Hertfordshire on 4 July and stealthily made her way by night towards her estates in East Anglia. Once certain that her brother had died, she proclaimed herself queen on 9 July, wrote to the privy council in London, demanding its allegiance, and made her base in Framlingham Castle. Catholics in East Anglia and elsewhere immediately rallied behind her, forming an impressive army.

Jane was proclaimed queen in London on the afternoon of 10 July, and escorted to the Tower with traditional ceremony. At first she attracted some support in strong Protestant areas of the country, but many thought she was usurping the throne. The crew of five royal ships, moored in Orwell harbour, mutinied "because of the disowning of Princess

Mary"; and when Northumberland led troops from London to combat Mary, he noticed that large crowds greeted his departure with sullen resentment and no "God-speeds".

Confronted with the prospect of civil war, Jane's supporters reconsidered their allegiance. During Northumberland's absence from London, his colleagues on the council defected one by one. On 19 July they published a proclamation recognising Mary as queen, and by that evening Jane and her husband were prisoners in the Tower. The next day Northumberland surrendered at Cambridge and proclaimed Mary queen. The crisis was over.

Mary wisely decided to restrict her reprisals, and most of those who signed the letters patent kept their positions in the state. Jane and her family were spared death, until her father participated in Wyatt's rebellion in early 1554; she and her husband were then brought to the scaffold. To satisfy any doubters, Mary's first parliament removed the taint of bastardy by declaring her parents' marriage valid. In a separate statute, it was declared that she had the same powers as a king. England's first ruling queen had successfully taken the throne.

How serious was the Catholic challenge to Elizabeth?

During Mary's reign, a few Protestant exiles had urged the Catholic Queen's deposition on grounds of her religion, tyranny and (in the case of John Knox) gender. When the Protestant Elizabeth assumed the throne, English Catholics behaved differently, recognising straight away her right to rule.

The immediate Catholic challenge to Elizabeth came from the Continent, where Henry II of France upheld the dynastic claim of his new daughter-in-law, Mary Queen of Scots. After Henry II's death in 1559, Mary – now also Queen of France – continued to maintain her claim by quartering the royal arms of England on her heraldic shields (combining the French and English coats of arms, with each given two quarters of the shield).

Even when she was forced to cease this practice, she consistently refused to ratify the Anglo-French Treaty of Edinburgh (1560) that denied her title to the English throne. She argued that the treaty also *implicitly* denied her right to the succession, but Sir William Cecil, Elizabeth's principal secretary and most influential councillor, concluded that she was still claiming to be the actual queen of England.

Initially, Mary received little or no support from English Catholics, who seemed content to wait until Elizabeth's marriage or death for the restoration of the Roman Church. Those who found it impossible to live under a Protestant went into exile.

Mary's eventual captivity in England and Protestant moves to exclude her from the succession changed the situation. In 1569, Catholic noblemen in the North raised a rebellion in her support; the following February, Pope Pius V issued a bull depriving Elizabeth "of her pretended claim to the kingdom"; and in 1571 the Ridolfi Plot was exposed, implicating the Pope, Philip II of Spain, Thomas fourth Duke of Norfolk, and Mary's adviser, John Leslie the Bishop of Ross, in a conspiracy to depose Elizabeth. Elizabeth responded with a wave of anti-Catholic measures, including a new Treasons Act (1571) which contained a clause making it high treason to deny her rightful title.

In fact, few English Catholics showed signs of disloyalty during the 1570s. As they well knew, any overt attack on Elizabeth's title would provoke fierce reprisals against the Catholic community and Scottish Queen. Nonetheless, Catholics consistently refused to comply with the state's demands that they conform. Furthermore, books by English Catholic exiles – such as the notorious *A Treatise of Treasons* (1572) – implied that Elizabeth could forfeit the loyalty and obedience of her subjects if she did not change her ways and allow, at the very least, toleration.

During the mid and late 1580s, Elizabeth's title was challenged more openly. There were a few small conspiracies (notably in the Throckmorton and Babington plots), and polemics printed abroad denied her right to rule. William Allen's *Admonition* (1588) was the most extreme, branding Elizabeth a bastard, the product of incest, a usurper, heretic and tyrant. The government's extensive use of spies, *agents provocateurs* and searches kept the Queen safe, however, while governmental propaganda tried to counteract Catholic diatribes. In 1584 English

Protestants signed a Bond of Association, devised to protect the Queen from an assassination attempt, and the following year Parliament passed an Act for the Queen's Surety.

Out of fear or sentiment, English Catholics remained loyal during the 1588 Armada scare. Some, like Viscount Montague, raised troops to resist a Spanish invasion; others adopted a wait-and-see policy. After the failed invasion, Catholic exiles – led by the Jesuit Robert Persons and layman Richard Verstegan – launched vitriolic attacks on Elizabethan policies and ministers but typically refrained from attacking the Queen's right to rule.

MARY QUEEN OF SCOTS

Mary became Queen of Scotland in December 1542, when she was six days old. Aged five, she was betrothed to Prince Edward of England, but her guardians broke the agreement, resulting in the so-called "Rough Wooing", a series of brutal English raids into Scotland.

In 1549 Mary was sent to France, where in April 1558 she married the dauphin, Francis, who became king in July 1559. Five months after his death in December 1560, Mary returned to Scotland, which was then Protestant. She ruled effectively, until her marriage in 1565 to her cousin Henry, Lord Darnley (also the great grandson of Henry VII), ignited political instability that resulted in his murder (1566), her forced abdication (1567) and flight to England (May 1568).

Over the next 19 years, Elizabeth kept Mary confined in castles within England. As a Catholic, she became the focus of plots. In February 1587 she was executed on a charge of treason after a tribunal found her guilty of involvement in the Babington Plot. ∎

On the whole, Catholics were awaiting Elizabeth's death and hoping for a successor who was either a Catholic or prepared to grant them toleration. But the Catholic community was not politically supine. Its networks in the North disseminated anti-Protestant material and had links with Scottish Catholics, the French Catholic League, lay Catholic exiles based in Flanders, and priests operating secretly in England. The Elizabethan government had sound reason to be watchful.

How did Elizabeth deal with the succession problem?

The last in her father's line, Elizabeth needed to marry and bear children to resolve the succession. Until a child was born – and especially in case one were not – a clear heir presumptive needed naming, preferably by the Queen in parliament. Otherwise, there would probably be a disputed succession and a destructive civil war on her death.

As matters stood when she came to the throne, there was a dangerous lack of clarity about who was next in line. Mary of Scotland and her supporters rejected Henry VIII's will, since it defied the principle of primogeniture in prioritising the Suffolk line. They also contested the will's legality, by alleging that Henry had not signed the document himself, as the 1544 statute required. Protestants, however, who opposed Mary's succession because of her religion and nationality, accepted the will as legal.

As an alternative to Mary, many Protestants initially promoted the claim of Katherine, the sister of Lady Jane Grey, of the Suffolk line. Elizabeth rejected this idea. Katherine had secretly married the Protestant Edward Seymour, Earl of Hertford, in December 1560 and immediately fallen pregnant. The lovers, unwisely, had not sought or secured the Queen's approval for their marriage and were consequently incarcerated in the Tower once Katherine could no longer hide her pregnancy. Despite their imprisonment, they were able to resume sexual relations, and Katherine delivered a second son in the Tower 18 months after the birth of the first. Following Elizabeth's wishes, a commission found that no proper marriage had taken place and the boys were therefore bastards.

After Katherine's death in January 1568, some Protestants favoured bringing her bastard sons into the succession. Others preferred Mary's son, James, who was being raised in Scotland by Protestant guardians and tutors. All leading Protestants wanted Elizabeth to name an heir and permit a new succession bill to pass through parliament that would exclude Mary. Throughout the reign, the succession question was openly introduced in parliament, discussed in pamphlets, and broached more obliquely in plays and other forms of literature.

Why did Elizabeth not resolve the succession by marrying? Many biographers and historians take the view that she never intended to take a husband, either for psychological reasons or because she feared a loss of power. This seems unlikely, though, because she showed a strong desire to marry Robert Dudley (later Earl of Leicester) in 1560 and Francis, Duke of Anjou, in 1579 – and a readiness to consider marriage to Archduke Charles of Austria and Henry, Duke of Anjou (later Henry III of France), if terms could be agreed. My own view is that strong hostility in England to all these suitors held her back from embarking on an unpopular choice, so keeping her single.

ENGLAND UNDER THE TUDORS

When Henry VII came to the throne in 1485, England's population was growing fast as the country recovered from the devastating Black Death of the mid-14th century and the periodic outbreaks of plague which followed it. Historians estimate that England had about 2.2 million people in 1485 and 4.1 million in 1601.

The rise in population led to price rises (because of the pressure of demand) and kept wages low (since labour was bountiful), making life harder for labourers and artisans. Poverty was an endemic problem of the Tudor period, causing concern to the governing classes who were fearful of crime, riots and wider unrest.

Most of the Tudors' subjects – more than 90% of the English population – lived in the countryside and worked in arable and/or pastoral farming. To profit from the thriving cloth industry, some large landowners – especially in the Midlands – were converting their arable land to pasture and building up large flocks of sheep. These

Elizabeth did not name a successor during the Scottish Queen's lifetime, because the question was so divisive. To her mind, Mary had the best right in blood. Elizabeth also disliked the Greys because of Jane's attempt to disinherit both her and her sister in 1553. But she knew Mary was unacceptable to most Protestants and consequently felt her best, indeed only, possible course was to protect her cousin's position by keeping the succession open. So she made sure that Katherine's sons remained legally bastards, by denying their father's efforts to make them legitimate, and she

landowners also began encroaching upon common land, and erecting fences or hedges to contain their sheep in the practice known as enclosure.

Meanwhile, the cities – London in particular – grew rapidly. London's population was about 50,000 in 1485 and quadrupled to an estimated 200,000 at the beginning of the 17th century. The increase was not a natural one, as death rates were high. It came about because of migration from rural areas: young men moving to the city in search of apprenticeships and women arriving to look for work in domestic or retail services. Most other towns had a population no larger than 5,000. (The few exceptions included Norwich and Bristol.)

London's success was due partly to its position as England's economic heart, partly because it was the site where parliament and the Inns of Court were based. During the Tudor era it developed into a thriving cultural centre. England in 1485 was on the cusp of an intellectual revolution thanks to the growing influence of humanist scholars who provided a classical education for the social elite. Humanist studies included Latin and Greek language prevented her parliaments from excluding Mary. Quite possibly, Elizabeth kept hidden her father's will; it certainly went missing so that it could not be inspected.

As for Mary's son, King James VI of Scotland, Elizabeth did not fully trust him. She therefore held out the succession as a reward for his loyalty and good behaviour. At the same time, she cleared his way to the throne by preventing any potential English rival from building up a power base. His English cousin, Arbella Stuart, was mainly confined to her maternal grandmother's house in Derbyshire

---

and literature, and emphasised the skill of rhetoric (the effective use of language for public argument). Leading humanists, such as Erasmus, also promoted classical languages and Hebrew in an attempt to recover the meaning of biblical texts and provide more accurate translations of the Bible than the Latin Vulgate, the late fourth-century translation then used by the Roman Catholic Church.

Humanists wanted reforms in Church and state. Erasmus and the clerics John Colet and John Fisher were just a few of those who called for an educated clergy, the removal of ecclesiastical corruptions, and bible-reading to be a crucial element in Christian piety.

England in 1485 was not as politically weak as Tudor propagandists liked to claim. It suited propagandists to portray Henry VII as the restorer of order after a period of strife and civil warfare. In reality, Edward IV had ruled in relative peace for 13 years: crown finances had recovered under the Yorkist King, who had managed his estates more efficiently than his predecessors. Indeed, Edward was the first king since Henry II not to leave debts on his death.

and kept unmarried.

At one level, Elizabeth dealt with the succession badly, since it remained a source of political instability until at least 1601. But would her endorsement of a candidate have ended the problem? Probably not! Had she supported the claim of Katherine Grey in the 1560s as many Protestants wanted, Mary's adherents at home and abroad would probably have intervened on her (Mary's) behalf. Equally, had Elizabeth later named the Protestant James VI as her heir, the Spanish King might well have supported a Catholic claimant

---

The problem of 'over-mighty' subjects had also been largely solved. The civil wars had reduced the number and power of the great magnates – a major cause of instability during the mid-15th century. The vast estates in the northern counties, which had once been held by the powerful Neville family, came into the hands of Edward's brother Richard, Duke of Gloucester who – during his two years as king (Richard III) – destroyed members of his extended royal family and seized their lands. As a result, Henry, on his accession, inherited vast estates and was the largest landowner in the realm.

Nonetheless, the civil wars had severely damaged the authority of kings. Although Edward IV died in his bed, the crown had changed hands violently five times from 1460 to 1485, and on three separate occasions with the help of foreign powers. The nobility, though weakened, remained the king's necessary partners in governing the country yet their allegiance to the crown could not be assumed.

Henry had every reason to feel insecure in 1485, despite his military victory and unopposed coronation. Added to these difficulties was the fact – and it was very much a fact – that his claim to the throne was weak. ■

more aggressively. As the 1553 crisis demonstrated, naming an heir was no guarantee of a smooth succession on the Queen's death.

Religious Reformations

How strong and popular was the English Church before the break with Rome?

In 1992, Eamon Duffy compellingly revealed the vibrancy and popularity of traditional religious beliefs and worship before Henry VIII's break with Rome.[*] As a result, historians now widely accept that there was little contemporary dissatisfaction with the doctrines, liturgy and devotional practices of the late-medieval Catholic Church, even though many churchgoers probably understood little of its complex theological teachings.

Since Duffy, historians have shown that the Church allowed a variety of Christian practices and did not impose a rigid orthodoxy on its members. Individuals expressed their piety in different ways: some, for example, emphasised saint worship, others the reading of devotional books. This toleration of a variety of opinions – or heterodoxy – can be seen as a reflection of the Church's strength: it was relaxed enough to allow its parishioners to gain spiritual

---

[*] Eamon Duffy, *The Stripping of the Altars: Traditional Religion in England, c.1400-c.1580* (New Haven, 1992).

satisfaction from privatised forms of worship and/or communal expressions of religious culture.

There is also now widespread agreement that relatively few heretics were present in England during the early 16th century. The drive of early Tudor bishops to eliminate Lollardy and Lutheranism is now seen as a sign of the bishops' reforming zeal rather than a reaction to any kind of serious threat to the Church.

Nonetheless, few historians are as bold as Richard Rex in dismissing Lollardy as virtually defunct and insignificant by the 1520s.[*] The number of English heretics may have been small and their beliefs somewhat vague, but in a few towns and villages there were religious communities which held unorthodox views and met to hear readings from an English Bible. Early Evangelicals, moreover, revived Lollard texts and showed deep respect for the Lollard tradition which became absorbed into English Protestantism by 1540.

As for the extent of abuses in the late-medieval Church and lay dissatisfaction with it, there is now considerable consensus about this, too. No historian today would paint a picture of a moribund institution ripe for reformation, as did A. G. Dickens in his influential *The English Reformation* (1967). Revisionist historians of the mid 1980s and 1990s stress instead the Church's strengths and dismiss the notion of rampant anti-clericalism on the eve of

---

[*] Richard Rex, *The Lollards* (Basingstoke, 2002).

the Reformation. Christopher Harper-Bill emphasises the high quality of early Tudor bishops, who proved able administrators of their dioceses as well as patrons of learning and charity, while Christopher Haigh maintains that the lower clergy met the spiritual and social needs of parishioners, who rarely complained about the quality of their

WHO BELIEVED WHAT?

Catholics: Christians who believed that to obtain salvation the faithful had to participate in the sacraments (especially baptism, penance and the Mass) and "works" (such as pilgrimages). Roman Catholics believed that the pope was the spiritual head of the Church, and that all priests should be celibate. Protestants called Catholics "papists".

Church papists: Catholics who were prepared to obey the law and attend Protestant church services (if only occasionally). Those who refused to attend were called "recusants".

Conservatives in religion: Catholics prepared to go along with Henry's break from Rome but resistant to many Protestant reforms.

Evangelicals: Reformers who emphasised the role of faith in salvation, the authority of Scripture, and the importance of preaching. They supported Henry VIII's attack on "superstitious practices" but did not, by then, reject Catholic sacramental beliefs.

Lollardy: A heretical movement derived from the 14th century translator of the Bible, John Wycliffe. Lollards stressed the primacy of Scripture and held unorthodox beliefs about the sacraments and priesthood.

priests or their financial exactions.

This revisionism, however, has itself been somewhat revised, with some modern historians once again pointing to fault-lines in the late medieval Church. George Bernard, for example, provides a balance sheet of what he calls its "vitality

* Christopher Harper-Bill, *The Pre-Reformation Church in England 1400-1530* (Harlow, 1989); Christopher Haigh, *English Reformations: Religion, Politics and Society under the Tudors* (Oxford, 1993).

Lutherans: Followers of Martin Luther, a German monk, who believed salvation was attainable not by "works" (such as the Mass, confession and pilgrimages) but simply by faith alone, that is faith in Christ's redeeming sacrifice on the Cross. They saw faith as a gift from God. Luther was excommunicated by Pope Leo X in 1520.

Nicodemites: the pejorative name for Protestants who outwardly conformed, under Mary I. The term refers to the biblical Pharisee Nicodemus, who would only visit Christ in secret.

Presbyterians: Puritans (see below) who wanted to abolish bishops and have churches run by ministers, elders and deacons. They were strongly influenced by John Calvin, who established a Presbyterian Church in Geneva.

Protestants: Christians who denied that "works" played any role in salvation. Believing in the supreme authority of Scripture, they rejected papal authority. Some Protestants were Lutheran; others followed the teachings of reformers like Calvin.

Puritans: A pejorative name given to Protestants who wanted the English Church to be purer and further reformed. Those called Puritans disapproved of "popish" ceremonies like ministers wearing vestments, the use of the cross in baptism and the ring in marriage, and kneeling at Holy Communion. Puritans led a godly lifestyle, regularly reading the Bible and listening to preaching. ■

and vulnerability".[*] Bernard sees no signs of an impending "Reformation" and rejects the Dickensian narrative that identified a crescendo of clerical abuses and lay anti-clericalism. But he believes there *were* endemic weaknesses in the Church, which made it vulnerable when it came under attack during the reign of Henry VIII.

The most pervasive weakness was a general worldliness. Bishops were regularly employed in royal service and had to display a magnificence that sat uneasily with Christian ideals. Cathedral staff were equally preoccupied with worldly affairs, since they had to be diocesan administrators and financial managers. The problem was not only that the upper clergy's lives could be open to criticism but that the Church was what Bernard dubs a "monarchical Church". Its leading clerics, therefore, found it very hard to come to the institution's defence when the King attacked it during the 1520s and 1530s.

As for the lower clergy, the problem was often human frailty. Many monastic and parish priests understandably had difficulty in living up to the high standards of spirituality and celibacy expected of them. Leading churchmen endeavoured to address the problem. The Dean of St Paul's, John Colet, famously cried out for the need to reform "the wicked life of priests" in an impassioned sermon before the southern convocation (the general assembly of the clergy from the Archdiocese of

[*] G.W. Bernard, *The Late Medieval English Church: Vitality and Vulnerability Before the Break with Rome* (New Haven, 2012).

Canterbury). Bishop John Fisher of Rochester, John Longland of Lincoln and Cardinal Wolsey closed down disreputable monasteries and diverted their endowments towards new educational projects.

Once again, however, we need to keep things in perspective – that some priests lacked a sense of vocation was hardly new. But after Henry VIII broke with Rome, Evangelicals seized upon scandals – especially within monastic houses – to justify their programme of more radical reforms.

There is no doubt that there were disputes between individuals and their priests: burial charges (known as mortuaries), tithes and other fees could cause bitter resentment and discord, even if the disputes were usually settled fairly amicably. Lawyers who practised "common law" disliked the church courts which took away some of their business, while MPs complained about the clergy's exemption from trial in common law courts (known as benefit of clergy). George Bernard argues, rightly, that lay anger over matters such as these did not amount to "anti-clericalism" or to a "bottom-up" push for reformation. They did, however, come to be exploited by Henry VIII and his propagandists when Henry decided to strike out against the independence and privileges of the Church.

Why did Henry VIII introduce religious change?

Henry did not begin life a Catholic and die a Protestant, nor did he establish a Protestant Church after his break with the papacy. What he did was move the English Church away from *some* Catholic beliefs (notably papal supremacy) and many traditional practices by dissolving the monasteries, licensing an English Bible, attacking the cult of saints, and banning ceremonies that he condemned as unscriptural or superstitious.

Contrary to popular myth, Henry consistently thought of himself as Catholic, denying the Lutheran doctrine of justification by faith alone and reaffirming orthodox teachings on the Mass, penance and clerical celibacy. He was still defending the existence of purgatory in the mid-1530s, and even if in *The King's Book* of 1543 he seemed less

THE PROCESS OF
HENRY VIII'S
REFORMATION

1531 Southern convocation recognises Henry as "Supreme Head of the Church of England" as far as the law of Christ allows.
1533 Act of Appeals.
1534 Act of Supremacy.
1536 Statute dissolving the lesser monasteries (worth under £200 per annum). Thomas Cromwell's injunctions (attacking superstition and idolatry). The Ten Articles (reformist statement of doctrine) issued by convocation.
1537 *The Bishops Book* (unacceptable to Henry).

sure – ordering people to "abstain from the name of purgatory and no more dispute or reason thereof" – he doesn't seem to have convinced himself. In his own will he left money for Masses to speed his soul through purgatory.

While historians acknowledge that Henry had a deep interest in theology, they disagree about his exact religious standpoint. George Bernard and Lucy Wooding see his views as perfectly coherent, maintaining that his reformation was an essentially "Erasmian process".* Erasmus was the Dutch Catholic priest and Christian humanist who had mounted literary attacks on "superstitious" practices and advocated that a vernacular Bible (i.e. one written in a language non-theologians could understand) be available to all Christians. The King

* Lucy Wooding, *Henry VIII* (London, 2008); G.W. Bernard, 'Henry VIII: "Catholicism without the Pope?"', *History*, 101 (2016), pp. 201-21.

1538 Cromwell's second set of injunctions.
1539 Publication of the Great Bible. Act of Six Articles (a statement of six points of Catholic doctrine, given statutory authority).
1543 Act for Advancement of True Religion (restricting bible-reading). *The King's Book* (orthodox on justification by faith but questioning purgatory).
1544 Introduction of the English Litany (petitionary prayers, excising portions dependent on the cult of saints). New English Primer (a devotional book containing prayers, psalms and liturgical extracts).
1545 The partial dissolution of the chantries (endowments which maintained priests to say Masses for the souls of named individuals). ∎

was a life-long admirer of Erasmus, according to Bernard and Wooding, and his religious practices and policy reflected Erasmian principles.

Other historians think this is over-simplifying the matter. Richard Rex argues that before the 1530s Henry venerated saints' relics and prayed at their shrines, practices which Erasmus attacked. After breaking with Rome, says Rex, Henry adopted theological positions which had been rejected by the humanist reformer: Henry's Erasmianism, in other words, "was both highly selective and utterly devoid of the master's subtlety and nuance".[*]

But while he may not have been a *consistent* Erasmian, Henry was undoubtedly influenced by Erasmus's writings. Furthermore, he and his propagandists leant heavily on the humanist's works when they were defending the religious reforms of the 1530s. Yet it is true that Henry was subject to other influences as well. Once he decided that *he* – not the pope – was the supreme head of the English Church, he took very seriously the traditional belief that Christian kings had a responsibility for the spiritual welfare of their subjects.

He saw himself as a David or Solomon, the theocratic kings of the Hebrew Bible with a divine mission to enforce the law of God and eradicate idolatry. It was with this in mind that he authorised the use of an English Bible, ordered the destruction of images that were objects of veneration, and sought

---

[*] Richard Rex, 'The Religion of Henry VIII', *The Historical Journal*, 57 (2014), pp. 1-32.

to establish a new formulary of faith for his Church.

Henry was no purist, though: politics and money played their part in shaping the nature of his Church. He rejected the theology of justification by faith alone largely because he believed that good works encouraged obedience and order. The taxation survey of 1535, revealing the huge wealth of the monasteries, encouraged – and perhaps caused – him to dissolve the smaller houses in 1536. The attack on the 202 larger monasteries that began in 1537 was triggered by the role of the monks in the northern insurrection known as the Pilgrimage of Grace. And the need for money to fund the French war explains the partial dissolution of the chantries in 1545.

But was Henry the sole architect of the religious reforms? Most historians think not. Key advisers, they argue, shaped both his thinking and the way his reforms were implemented. Eric Ives, for example, sees Anne Boleyn as an important influence both in the denial of papal supremacy and in the promotion of an English Bible. Maybe so, but her role is difficult to determine.

The argument that the two Thomases were important influences is much more convincing. Almost certainly it was Thomas Cromwell who conceived the strategy of effecting the break with Rome through parliamentary statute. Moreover, as "Vice-regent in Spirituals" from 1535, he helped steer England towards reformation – overseeing the dissolution of the monasteries, drafting the injunctions of 1536 and 1538, and protecting

Evangelicals in London and elsewhere. His execution in 1540 was rightly seen at the time as a severe setback to the evangelical cause. As for Thomas Cranmer, he discussed theology with the King, introduced religious change in his diocese, and used his patronage to promote reformist clergy. Religious conservatives also played their part. Bishops Cuthbert Tunstall and Stephen Gardiner advised on the Act of Six Articles and convinced Henry that Cromwell was a heretic.

This is not to say that Henry VIII was a puppet of factions, whether evangelical or conservative. But nor did he operate in a vacuum, untouched by the opinions and initiatives of men and women with access to his ear and influence in the dioceses. He listened to the proposals of the Evangelicals, but also to the arguments of conservatives who alerted him to the danger of England falling into dangerous heresy.

Religious beliefs were in flux both in England and on the Continent, and Henry's theologians and laymen fiercely contested points of doctrine. So his Reformation lacked clear direction and was by no means entirely coherent. In 1541, for example, he re-established some traditional feast days of saints while revoking others as based on superstition. Henry did not, as many believe, move inexorably towards the Protestantism introduced during the reign of his son, even though he prepared the ground for it. His Reformation was *sui generis,* unique and idiosyncratic, the product of the King's own preferences and uncertainties.

Why were there so many changes in religion between 1547 and 1559?

As religious change in England was a top-down phenomenon, the easy answer is that the different beliefs of the Tudor monarchs explain the dramatic changes in England's religion: the Reformed Protestantism of the boy-king Edward, the Roman Catholicism of Mary, the conservative Protestantism of Elizabeth. But this explanation is far too simple, ignoring political power struggles and the influence of continental developments.

The Edwardian Reformation was the work of a small clique. It happened because Henry VIII had imprisoned the conservative Duke of Norfolk in 1546 and because his final will excluded Bishop Gardiner from the regency council. The absence of these two figures enabled Edward Seymour, shortly to be created Duke of Somerset, to mount a successful palace coup which made him Lord Protector. Somerset was evangelical by inclination and immediately began working with Cranmer to introduce religious reforms. That their measures did not go further before 1550 was because of the regime's caution in the face of a conservative parliament at home and the need to keep peace with the Catholic Charles V.

When Somerset fell from power in autumn 1549, there was a chance the conservatives might seize control. They failed to do so. John Dudley, Earl of Warwick, (later Duke of Northumberland) forged a political alliance with Cranmer to thwart them. Seven traditionalist bishops were deprived of their posts, reducing the conservative majority in the House of Lords. It was full steam ahead for reform, especially as Edward's Protestant zeal was becoming increasingly apparent. Ambitious royal servants became committed to reformation in order to keep his confidence.

Three theologians – Cranmer, Hugh Latimer and Nicholas Ridley – were the driving force behind the changes. But Charles V's victory over German Protestant princes at Mühlberg in April 1547 resulted in the arrival of continental reformers as religious exiles. Through the influence of these exiles, English Protestants moved away from the Lutheran teachings that had been influential in

THE EDWARDIAN REFORMATION

1547 Royal Injunctions (ordering parochial destruction of superstitious images); Cranmer's Homilies (official sermons embodying Protestant doctrines); and Erasmus' *Paraphrases* (commentaries on the New Testament) ordered to appear in parish churches. Repeal of Act of Six Articles. Act dissolving all chantries. Act permitting communion in both kinds (wafer and wine) for the laity.
1548 Removal of all images from churches.
1549 Act legalising clerical marriage. New Prayer Book. Act of Uniformity.
1550 New Protestant Ordinal (for ordination of priests and consecration of bishops). Proclamation ordering destruction of images in one's personal possession. Order to remove altars.

evangelical circles under Henry VIII towards the theology and form of worship we now term Reformed.

The most prominent theologians who took shelter in England were Martin Bucer and Peter Martyr Vermigli, both from Strasbourg. Installed as Professors of Theology at the Universities of Cambridge and Oxford respectively, the two professors promoted Protestantism and influenced Cranmer's theology. All these reformers had moved away from Luther's theology on the Lord's Supper.

The accession of Mary to the throne ensured a return to Rome. Under duress she had accepted the schism in 1536 but had bravely defied her brother's order to cease having the Mass celebrated in her household. She then became convinced that papal

---

1552 Second Prayer Book. 42 Articles of Faith (Cranmer's statement of faith for the English Church).

One key feature of the Edwardian Reformation was its so-called iconoclasm (the wide-ranging destruction of religious images and icons). The other was Cranmer's two Prayer Books. They introduced two new daily services in English, in which were included readings from the Old and New Testaments and prayers derived from Scripture. The 1549 book retained much of the traditional ceremonial, vestments and ornaments; it also hedged its bets on the theology of the Lord's Supper, allowing belief in Christ's bodily presence. The 1552 book was openly radical, making drastic revisions to the communion service. It now took place at a table (not an altar), used ordinary bread (not a wafer) and denied the bodily presence of Christ. Although kneeling was still permitted, the so-called "Black Rubric" denied any adoration of the bread and wine. Some vestments were retained. ■

authority was essential in order to protect the Mass and Catholic teachings. The seven traditionalist bishops who had been deprived of their posts for opposing the Edwardian reforms supported the restoration of papal power for the same reason.

Mary encountered little parliamentary opposition to the repeal of the Edwardian religious statutes but many MPs resisted the repeal of Henry's anti-papal legislation. Catholics and Protestants alike had bought ex-ecclesiastical lands and feared these now might be confiscated. Only after Cardinal Pole did a deal with the Pope to allow lay land-holders to retain their newly acquired lands did Mary's parliament in November 1554 repeal all the religious statutes enacted since 1529, restoring papal authority.

In the past, historians have criticised Mary's restoration as "sterile", with an emphasis on coercion rather than the revival of Catholic spirituality. Historians today reject this, and rightly so.* Far from being insular and uncreative, Mary's Catholic Reformation was influenced by new thinking and practices from abroad. Marian printers produced a steady flow of devotional books containing new prayers; Pole proposed the establishment of diocesan seminaries for the clergy; and the bishops planned a new Catholic translation of the Bible.

Mary's Catholic Reformation died with the

---

* See Susan Doran and Thomas S. Freeman (eds), *Mary Tudor: Old and New Perspectives* (Basingstoke, 2011).

42-year-old Queen. Had she produced a child or managed to exclude her half-sister Elizabeth from the succession, England would have remained Roman Catholic. The restoration of the Mass had

CONFESSIONAL DIVISIONS

	Roman Catholic	Lutheran	Reformed
Doctrines	justification by faith and works	justification by faith alone	predestination
	7 sacraments	2 sacraments	2 sacraments
	belief in purgatory	no purgatory	no purgatory
Lord's Supper	communion in one kind (wafer) for the laity	communion in both kinds	communion in both kinds
	intercession	no intercession	no intercession
	bodily presence of Christ	bodily presence	only spiritual presence
ornaments	images, roods	some images	no images
	vestments	some vestments	no vestments
	altar	altar/table	table
	wafer at Mass	wafer at Mass	bread at communion
authority	papal supremacy, apostolic tradition, scripture	scripture alone	scripture alone

considerable popular backing, and those Protestants who were not burned were forced into exile, underground cells or outward conformity. Yet there was no opposition to Elizabeth's accession in November 1558, even though few doubted that she would once again break with Rome and introduce religious change. The alternative to Elizabeth was Mary Stewart who would bring England into a French Empire.

When parliament met in January 1559, Elizabeth's government introduced bills of supremacy and uniformity. The legislation faced stiff opposition from the Catholic majority in the House of Lords, passing there only after two Catholic bishops were arrested on trumped-up charges during the Easter recess. One important amendment was made to the supremacy bill: Elizabeth's title was Supreme Governor (not Head) of the Church. Even so, all but one of the Catholic bishops refused to take the Oath of Supremacy and were consequently replaced by Protestants, many of whom had recently returned from exile in Reformed cities of Europe.

How did parishioners react to religious change?

Historians now agree that the Reformation was a long drawn out, even painful process. Although some parishioners welcomed the religious changes, most people were either indifferent or hostile, compelled to make difficult choices about how to react. But while there was some resistance, the majority outwardly conformed to preserve communal harmony or advance their own personal interests (such as their hold on church property through plunder or purchase).

The general pattern was that the greater the distance from London and the main trade routes, the longer it took for Protestant ideas to take hold. Towns – where there was also a higher degree of literacy – were more likely to accept and promote Protestant reform than small rural communities. In some places there was compromise, collaboration and a degree of harmony when change was introduced; in others, there were tensions between enthusiastic Protestants and reluctant church papists (who conformed but identified themselves as Catholic).

Governments used a mixture of coercion and propaganda to get their way. Evangelicals under Henry and Protestants under Edward resorted to preachers and printers to convert people, but the limitations of this approach were revealed during Mary's reign, when most people attended Mass without protest and voluntarily returned images to their churches. Some conformists were so-called "Nicodemites" (outwardly conforming while hiding their Protestant faith from the government) but most parishioners seem to have been relieved at the return of Catholic beliefs and worship, raising money to furnish their churches with altars, roods, and ornaments necessary for the Mass. Studies show that by 1557 most parishes had acquired an altar, vestments and missals.

Local gentry and townsfolk who had been compliant in accepting the Edwardian reforms also collaborated in the arrest and burning of some 300 Protestants between February 1555 and July 1558. Among the victims was the 66-year-old Thomas Cranmer who was sent to the stake in March 1556 even though he had signed a statement recanting his Protestant beliefs. But what should have been a propaganda victory for the Catholic Church turned into a fiasco. Just before taking his position on the pyre, Cranmer recanted his recantation, and once the fire was lit he stretched his hand into the flames saying "this hand hath offended".

Otherwise the burnings took place without serious incident. There were no riots nor attempts to rescue prisoners. Only in London and Colchester did the authorities fear disturbances but, even in these two cities, all was quiet.

During the early decades of Elizabeth's reign, committed Protestants were a small minority in the parishes. The majority were simply conformists or else church papists. Church papistry was sustained by Marian priests who remained in their parishes and kept alive Catholic traditions as best they could. Rather than active conversions, it was generational change that brought about Protestantism's success under Elizabeth. Over time, the Marian priests died to be replaced by newly ordained Protestant clerics.

Their parishioners – exposed to the 1559 Prayer Book, the English Bible, the Book of Homilies, John Foxe's *Acts and Monuments*, and a diet of Protestant sermons – found their memory of Catholic beliefs and practices beginning to fade, while their children had no experience of the "old religion".

Nonetheless, plenty of church papists clung to their faith, living a kind of double life. They occasionally – and grudgingly – attended church on Sundays, but not communion, and they internalised their devotions at home (using, for example, rosary beads and devotional books). Those who were gentry gave succour to the seminary priests and Jesuits who clandestinely entered England from the late 1570s onwards. More than 70 hiding places have been found where priests were kept, not all of them in the households of recusants.

On occasions, the papists who clung to their faith were troublemakers, disrupting services, and sometimes they moved into full-blown recusancy, refusing to attend weekly services. These recusants tended to be women: on the whole, Catholic men conformed, anxious to preserve their lives and property. It was easier for wives to rebel because women could find credible excuses for staying at home on Sundays and married women held no property so could not be fined. But the numbers were small. Historians estimate that by Elizabeth's death only about 1.5% of the population were recusants (some 40,000 people), though perhaps as many as one in four remained church papists.

TEN FACTS ABOUT THE TUDORS

1.
Henry VII never knew his father, Edmund, Earl of Richmond, who died of plague nearly three months before his son's birth. When he was four, Henry was separated from his mother, Margaret Beaufort, and brought up as a ward by a guardian in Raglan Castle in Wales until he was 14 and forced to live abroad.

2.
Henry VIII's elder brother, Arthur, was named after the mythical British king of Welsh descent, whom the Tudors claimed as an ancestor. Prince Arthur was born and baptised in Winchester, a town which was believed to be the site of Camelot. A replica Arthurian Round Table, originally constructed in the 13th century, still hangs in the Great Hall of Winchester Castle. Henry VIII, who also identified himself with the mythical Arthur, had the table repainted in its present form.

3.
The future Henry VIII was the barely noticed second son until the death of Prince Arthur. Unusually for a boy he was brought up with his two sisters and he was only set up as a prince in court at the age of 13 in 1504.

4.

At his accession in 1509, Henry VIII was tall, slim and athletic. But in 1536 he suffered a severe jousting accident which left him with a nasty and painful varicose ulcer in his leg. This led to infections, fevers and the discharge of putrid pus. Unable to take exercise, Henry grew obese and by 1541 his waist measured 54 inches and his chest 57 inches. In his last years, he had to be winched on to his horse.

5.

Far from being a weak and consumptive boy, Edward VI was relatively healthy and strong until he contacted measles in 1552. He rode well and loved hunting, archery and jousting.

6.

Mary took as much delight in clothes as her sister. In September 1553 Henry II of France was told that she should receive a gift of clothing "because she is... one of those ladies who takes the greatest pleasure in clothes".

7.

In October 1562, Elizabeth contracted smallpox and became so seriously ill that it was feared she would die. Although not too badly scarred, she used a cream of white lead and vinegar as cosmetics to hide the marks left by smallpox and give her face its fashionable white complexion. Her gentlewoman Lady Mary Sidney, who had nursed her during the illness, caught the disease and was badly disfigured.

8.
Elizabeth loved physical activities, especially walking, riding, hunting, and dancing (which was also considered "an exercise of the body"). The court would join her in these activities until close to the end of her life.

9.
Boys in Tudor schools learned to read from "hornbooks". Pages displaying the alphabet and religious material were attached to wooden boards and covered with a transparent sheet of cow horn (hence the name). They were affordable and durable, able to survive years of use by young boys.

10.
New to Elizabethan London were commercial playhouses that put on plays throughout the year and charged an entrance fee. Most of these purpose-built theatres were sited in the East End of the City or in Southwark on the south bank of the River Thames, because the City authorities disliked the theatre on social and religious grounds.

Opposite: Portrait of Henry VIII by Hans Holbein the Younger

Why were Protestants critical of the Elizabethan Church?

It is a mistake to see the Elizabethan Church as a *via media* or half-way house between Catholicism and Protestantism. The 1559 Prayer Book embodied Protestant teachings and renounced the Mass; the 39 Articles of Faith of 1563 expressed doctrines on predestination and communion that were Reformed; and the interiors of most parish churches were denuded of images, wall-paintings and altars. If the settlement was a middle way at all, it was between the Lutheran and Reformed branches of Protestantism.

From the outset, though, most committed Protestants – especially those who had been Marian exiles in Reformed communities – thought Catholic influence remained far too strong and were

PENAL LAWS AGAINST CATHOLICS

The Elizabethan government claimed it did not persecute Catholics but just prosecuted those who were seditious. However, Catholics – especially recusants – unquestionably came under considerable pressure:

1559 Act of Uniformity imposed a fine of 12d for missing church services.
1571 Statute ruled that the receipt of "superstitious" items, blessed by the pope or his priests, would lead to forfeiture of lands and goods.
1581 Statute made it treason to attempt to convert the Queen's subjects and increased recusancy fines to a crippling

dissatisfied with the Elizabethan Prayer Book. Some of its prayers, they felt, failed to reflect fully the theology of predestination as understood in Reformed Churches. Committed Protestants objected especially to the prayers at baptism and burial services. They also condemned various rituals and rubrics as "popish". Causing most offence were the sign of the cross at baptism and kneeling at communion.

Dissatisfaction with the Prayer Book led some zealous Protestant ministers to omit parts they found offensive. But Elizabeth wasn't having that. In 1565 Matthew Parker, the Archbishop of Canterbury – encouraged by the Queen – ordered total conformity. His insistence that ministers wear a white surplice and four-cornered clerical hat during services and the cope (a long mantle or cloak) at communion, provoked the "vestiarian

---

£20 a month.
1585 Statute made it treason for any priests ordained abroad since 1559 to enter England. Harbouring a priest was a felony, punishable by death.
1587 Recusants who defaulted on their fines could have two-thirds of their land seized.
1593 Statute restricted movements of recusants.

Under Elizabeth, about 189 Catholics were executed for treason (some 130 of whom were priests). Between 1581 and 1592 some £45,000 was collected in recusancy fines. Yet recusants were not marginalised, and many evaded fines because of local sympathisers. Although periodically removed from county offices, a surprising number of Catholics continued to hold important positions (like magistrates and commissioners) even in Protestant areas like Essex. ■

controversy", a dispute over non-conformity that raged acrimoniously for two years in print, the universities and parishes.

Those who refused to obey Parker – newly labelled "Puritans" by their opponents – justified their non-conformity by appealing to the Scriptures and their consciences. They also argued that the retention of "Romish rags" (priests' garments) would prevent "simple" people from understanding that all popery was intrinsically evil. On the other side, conformists asserted that royal authority was supreme in all matters indifferent to faith ("adiaphora"). Additionally, they defended clerical dress on the grounds that it would ease the road to conversion by showing continuity with the past.

Elizabeth eventually retreated on the necessity for copes in parish churches, but still insisted on the surplice and clerical hat. She also stalled further reformation by repeatedly preventing religious bills, which attempted to remove "popery" and encourage preaching, from passing through parliament. Puritans complained bitterly that the bishops and even the Queen were failing to implement God's word. The result was that a small radical group of Puritans began to advocate Presbyterianism.

Many Protestants hoped for better times when the Queen promoted Edmund Grindal to the Archdiocese of Canterbury in December 1575. Known as a zealous reformer, he was thought likely to turn a blind eye to the diversity of Protestant religious practice. But within 18 months Elizabeth had suspended him from office. His offence was his refusal to ban meetings (called "prophesyings") that were designed to train better preachers. Elizabeth had ordered their suppression because Puritans were known to preach at these meetings. As Grindal's successor, Elizabeth appointed the vehemently anti-presbyterian, and anti-puritan John Whitgift.

Supported by a new generation of like-minded bishops, Whitgift mounted a campaign to force ministers to subscribe to several conformist articles or lose their livings. Some 300-400 were initially suspended for refusing to endorse the Prayer Book without reservation. When prominent lay Protestants (including privy councillors) remonstrated, however, Whitgift backed down and reluctantly allowed limited subscription. So diversity in liturgical practice continued.

Whitgift proved more successful in attacking the nascent Presbyterian movement in England during the late 1580s and early 1590s. In imprisoning its leaders, destroying its presses, and uprooting its networks, he and other bishops were aided by two circumstances: the deaths of a number of sympathetic patrons of Puritans; and the growing radicalism of the Presbyterians and Separatists, which lost them the protection of other moderate and influential friends.

By 1603, the critics of the Elizabethan Church were temporarily silenced. But they found their voice again on James I's accession. Within months,

Puritans and Presbyterians organised a petitioning campaign in the hope that they could convince the new King to introduce wide-ranging ecclesiastical reform.

How dangerous were Puritans?

Elizabeth was certain that Puritans of all hues were dangerous to Church and state. Their zeal and programme of reform, she believed, threatened Church unity by alienating church-papists, traditionalists and lukewarm Protestants. The

WHO WERE THE PURITANS?

Around 1564, the word "Puritan" was coined as a pejorative term levelled at the non-conforming Protestant clergy. Soon it was being used more indiscriminately as an insult for men and women thought to be excessively "pious". Hence the historian Patrick Collinson's description of Puritanism as "not a thing identifiable in itself, but one half of a stressful relationship".

Puritans were not very different from other Protestants, even their conformist enemies. They shared the Reformed view of faith, were equally anti-papal, and likewise abominated idolatry.

So most historians define Puritans loosely as "hotter sorts of Protestant", lay people and clerics who lived more intense spiritual lives than their protestant neighbours. Their voluntary regimen of personal and communal devotions included "gadding" to sermons, godly reading, psalm-singing, *ex tempore* prayer, fasting and spiritual meditation. Styling themselves the "godly", they disobedience of non-conforming ministers she understandably treated as a challenge to royal authority and, implicitly, to royal supremacy. During the controversy over clerical dress, Puritan justifications for disobedience seemed to echo the subversive theories advanced by Marian exiles in the 1550s. As for Presbyterians and Separatists, they were in Elizabeth's eyes subversive sects.

Not all Elizabeth's councillors shared this broad-brush approach. Many made a distinction between moderates and radicals. The Earl of Leicester, Sir William Cecil and Sir Francis Walsingham were built up strong networks of sociability among themselves.

Peter Lake places them on a spectrum within the Church that ranged from church papists, "avant-garde" churchmen, through conformist Calvinists, to moderate Puritans and radical Puritans. Alec Ryrie, on the other hand, finds little distinction between Puritans and conformists. "Puritan," he writes, "is better used as an adjective than a noun" to describe "earnest" religious behaviour."

Many Puritans were also part of a political movement, pursuing the goal of thorough-going reformation according to the dictates of scripture. Yet they disagreed about how far that reformation should go. The most moderate remained prepared to accept the rule of the bishops, the more radical were Presbyterian, while the most extreme wanted to separate from the ungodly and worship in their own congregations, and so were known as Separatists. ■

*   Patrick Collinson, *The Birthpangs of Protestant England* (Basingstoke, 1988).
**   Peter Lake, 'Anti-Puritanism: The Structure of a Prejudice', in Kenneth Fincham and Peter Lake (eds), *Religious Politics in Post-Reformation England* (Woodbridge, 2006), pp. 80-97; Alec Ryrie, *Being Protestant in Reformation Britain* (Oxford, 2013).

just a few of the influential patrons of moderate Puritans, agreeing with much of their reforming programme and considering them the main fighting force against popery. These nobles even gave support to leading presbyterian divines – like John Field, Walter Travers, Thomas Cartwright and Laurence Chaderton – though they distanced themselves from the most radical.

What do historians think? For the most part, they agree with the Queen and Whitgift that Puritans were a danger to the unity of the Church. They were also a propaganda gift for Catholics, exposing divisions within the Protestant Church and eroding the Queen's image as a godly Deborah (the Old Testament Judge). But most historians doubt that MPs with puritan sympathies were anything more than a nuisance in parliament, while only in a few parishes were Puritans dangerous. Though activists in striving for a godly ministry and moral discipline, they were not trouble-makers and usually lived in peace with the less godly while keeping a social distance from the profane.

Presbyterianism was another matter. As Peter Lake has shown, it was essentially subversive.[*] First, the appeal that presbyterian polemicists made to popular opinion on matters of state was dangerous for an authoritarian government. In spite of its title,

---

[*] Peter Lake, 'Puritanism, (Monarchical) Republicanism, and Monarchy; or John Whitgift, Antipuritanism, and the "Invention" of Popularity', *Journal of Medieval and Early Modern Studies,* 40 (2010), pp. 463-95.

the presbyterian tract of 1572, *An Admonition to Parliament,* was intended for a public readership; so was the *Marprelate Tracts* of 1588-9, which wittily and irreverently attacked the bishops. Second, a presbyterian system, if imposed, would undermine the monarch by ending the royal supremacy and submitting rulers to "the scripturally informed advice of the godly clergy" in secular as well as spiritual matters. It would also dismantle society's hierarchical structures since a godly elite would assume responsibility for local governance and discipline.

During the 1570s and 1580s, an inchoate presbyterian organisation was putting down roots in local communities. Ministers from different parishes were coming together to attend underground conferences, known as "classes", in London, East Anglia, the East Midlands, Essex and possibly elsewhere. Unfortunately, historians only have detailed records of the "classes" held at Dedham in Essex, where a dozen or more clerics met semi-secretly about once a month between 1582 and 1589 in the houses of ministers and sympathetic laymen to discuss pastoral and regulatory issues. Since they were assuming functions that properly belonged to bishops and archdeacons, this activity was seen as a form of embryonic presbyterianism.

Despite its potential danger, the presbyterian movement never spread sufficiently to make it an *actual* danger to Church and state. Bills to abolish the bishops and introduce a presbyterian system of church government got nowhere in parliament. Moreover, the investigations and arrests initiated in 1589 after the publication of the *Marprelate Tracts* rendered the movement impotent until the accession of James I.

Government, politics and protest

Did the Tudors introduce innovations in Government?

There are really two questions here. Did Henry VII introduce fundamental changes in government rather than simply build on the work of the Yorkist Kings? And was there, as Sir Geoffrey Elton maintained, a "Tudor Revolution in Government"?

Traditionally, historians have emphasised the continuity between Yorkist and early Tudor government. Henry VII followed Edward IV in using "chamber finance", whereby the chamber in the royal household displaced the exchequer as the principal financial institution managing the royal estates and overseeing national taxation. The sources of income were largely the same: "ordinary" income from the royal demesne, feudal dues, and customs; "extraordinary" income from parliamentary tenths and fifteenths (a form of taxation levied on lands and other possessions, known as movables, paid by communities rather than individuals).

Like Richard III, Henry VII would not allow his office-holders to be retained by any other lord, thereby eroding the power of the nobility. Both the Yorkist and early Tudor courts were magnificent, influenced by the chivalric and courtly practices of the dukes of Burgundy and kings of France. Under both dynasties, the court was the magnet for the ruling elites and the forum for the distribution of patronage. There was also continuity in the personnel of Henry's councillors: 30 had served under Yorkist kings.

Nonetheless, while building on Yorkist precedents, Henry VII introduced important institutional changes. The Yorkists had used Justices of the Peace, but Henry VII was responsible for more than 21 statutes that extended their powers and responsibilities. JPs were to become the mainstay of Tudor government, not only in trying criminal cases at Quarter Sessions but also in carrying out local administrative tasks (such as controlling alehouses, investigating births of bastards, and regulating economic activity). Under Henry, the Star Chamber, whose judges were normally privy councillors, emerged as a separate court of law, hearing cases that concerned public disorder, private disputes about property rights, and the enclosure of land.

At court, Henry in 1485 instituted a new royal

bodyguard, wearing Tudor livery, which was in continual attendance in the chamber. Finally, he relied upon a new kind of government administrator, both at court and in the provinces: these new public servants were legally trained gentry, and their presence had the effect of increasingly marginalising the nobility.

G.R. Elton's famous thesis is that Thomas Cromwell brought in a revolution in government, transforming England from a medieval to a modern state. While Cromwell was in power during the 1530s, said Elton, England became a unified, independent sovereign state ruled by a constitutional monarch through national and bureaucratic institutions.

Elton's claims, however, have been largely discredited. He exaggerated Cromwell's influence, particularly over the break with Rome. The reforms of the 1530s were not "a planned exercise in statecraft", as he suggested, but a pragmatic response to the political problems of the time. And in emphasising "bureaucratic" institutions Elton failed to appreciate that post-Cromwellian government and politics remained highly personal and informal, whether centred at court, in the privy council or at local level. As Norman Jones explains, Tudor government was "a set of interlocking chains of local and regional authorities that tangled and crossed all the way to the royal court".[*] In other

---

[*] Norman Jones, *Governing by Virtue: Lord Burghley and the Management of Elizabethan England* (Oxford, 2015).

Edward VI (1537 - 1553)

words, it was unwieldy with overlapping jurisdictions, weak communications, and powerful lords – characteristics that are hardly features of a modern state.

Nonetheless, the changes that occurred under Henry VIII were important. The privy council, which came into being some time between 1536 and 1540, remained a key instrument of government – with executive as well as advisory functions – until Elizabeth's death. The courts of wards and liveries (established in 1540 with responsibility for collecting feudal dues and overseeing the crown's rights over wardship) survived until 1645. The 1536 (first) Act of Union, which reorganised Wales into shires with JPs and extended common law to the region, lasted into the 20th century. Nor should we forget a major reform introduced by Wolsey: the subsidy – a tax on individuals not communities – which was more flexibly assessed than fifteenths and tenths.

There were few significant changes after Henry's death, though there was one worth noting: the establishment of a system of lord lieutenancies in the counties. The roots of this lay in Edward's reign, when lieutenants were appointed annually to supervise the counties with authority over JPs, and under Mary, when appointments were made for certain counties at times of emergency. When England prepared for war in 1585, Elizabeth's government systematised lieutenancies: in most cases one lieutenant – usually a nobleman – was based in each county (occasionally there were two), assisted by a number of deputies who were senior members of the resident gentry. This administrative development proved successful and has lasted, albeit in a more ceremonial form, to the present day.

Did parliament become more important in the 16th century?

The 16th century is rightly considered an important period in the history of parliament. For one thing, it was only in the 1530s that parliamentary statutes were accepted, for the first time, as taking precedence over all other laws which dealt with Church and state.

Furthermore, it was under the Tudors that

parliament began to act and organise itself in ways which would be familiar to us in modern times. Its procedures were formalised, with the introduction of clear rules of debate, the reading of a bill three times before voting, and the sending of bills to committees for proper scrutiny. For the first time, proceedings were formally recorded: a continuous set of journals was kept for the Lords from 1510 and the Commons from 1547. And storage space, both in the Commons and in the Lords, was set aside to keep these records safe.

The composition of the two Houses changed significantly, too. Following the dissolution of the monasteries, the 31 mitred abbots no longer sat in the Lords, so lay peers came to outnumber the Lords Spiritual. In the Commons – permanently situated after 1549 in St Stephen's Chapel – the number of MPs grew from 296 to 462, an increase that enhanced the House's status as a point of contact between the crown and local regions. The wider nation, moreover, was increasingly kept informed about parliamentary business, as statutes (with their long preambles justifying the act) and speeches (particularly those of Elizabeth) were copied, edited and printed for wider dissemination.

But we need to keep the changes in perspective. The enhanced authority of parliament did *not* mean England became a limited monarchy. On the contrary, parliamentary sovereignty gave greater authority than ever to the monarch, whose will could be expressed through legislation. Monarchs could and did put pressure on parliaments to pass the laws they wanted. They managed parliament by use of the speaker, privy councillors sitting in the Commons and, as a last resort, the detention of troublesome MPs. All statutes, of course, had to have royal approval.

It is worth remembering, too, Conrad Russell's famous dictum that the early-modern parliament was an event not an institution.* Parliament met irregularly and only on the initiative of the monarch who also had the power to dissolve or prorogue it. In her 45-year reign, Elizabeth summoned just 13 sessions, each lasting only around 10 or 11 weeks. Parliamentary activity was also circumscribed under the Queen. The Lords and Commons discussed more than 950 legislative proposals and enacted more than 400 laws, but their freedom to introduce bills concerning political and religious matters was restricted. As Elizabeth warned at the opening of the 1593 Parliament, the freedom "to say yea or no to bills" did not include the right "to speak... of all causes", nor "to frame a form of religion, or a state of government".

Under Elizabeth, parliament was frequently a centre for political dissent, with MPs expressing trenchant views about the succession, Mary of Scotland, religion, and monopolies. There may not have been a well-organised puritan opposition but

---

* Conrad Russell, *Unrevolutionary England, 1603–1642* (London, 1990).

puritan MPs certainly made their presence felt, and in all sorts of ways.

Patrick Collinson points out that they organised political campaigns to petition the Queen in parliament to remedy abuses in the Church in 1576, 1581, 1584 and 1586. Nicholas Tyacke argues that Puritans were behind much parliamentary agitation concerning Mary and the succession. And David Dean calls the monopolies debate of 1601 "the most significant outburst of opposition in any Elizabethan parliament", unleashing "remarkable assertions of parliament's power over the royal prerogative".[*]

It should not be thought, though, that this kind of parliamentary activity was either entirely new or far-reaching. Some late medieval parliaments had equally taken on a political role, criticising royal policies, even impeaching crown servants. In no sense did an opposition emerge in Elizabethan sessions that drove forward the cause of parliamentary liberty and power. Historians today all agree that there was no straight line between the tensions within Elizabeth's parliaments and the struggles that ended in the English Civil War.

---

[*] Patrick Collinson, *The Elizabethan Puritan Movement* (London, 1967); Nicholas Tyacke, 'The Puritan Paradigm of English Politics, 1558–1642', *The Historical Journal*, 53 (2010), pp. 527–50; David Dean, *Law-Making and Society in Late Elizabethan England: The Parliament of England 1584-1601* (Cambridge, 1996).

How important was factional in-fighting in Tudor political life?

Political factions under the Tudors tended to be informal and fluid groupings, coming together for particular reasons, often temporarily. The men and women within them were linked by patronage, or family interests, or shared political or religious beliefs. Monarchs could keep these groupings in check or balance, but in certain circumstances – a weak monarch, say, or divisive policies – factions could result in in-fighting at court, even coups.

There has been fierce debate about the role of factions during Henry VIII's reign. David Starkey and Eric Ives believe they were important as a driving force of political life, with rival factions operating at Henry's court from the mid-1520s until the King's death. Differing over policy – most obviously religious policy – these loosely-formed groups of men and women competed for influence over the King to advance their political agendas and patronage needs. They put their friends in the privy chamber, dangled attractive ladies of the court before Henry's eyes, and spread malicious gossip about their enemies.

According to these historians, the result was not only shifts in royal policy but also the downfalls of Wolsey, Anne Boleyn and Cromwell. Factional intrigue did not stop there. In 1543 conservatives plotted to tar Cranmer with the brush of heresy, and in 1546 they attempted to incriminate suspected

Evangelicals at court, especially Queen Katherine Parr. The 1543 plot failed because of Henry's affection for Cranmer; the 1546 conspiracy was unsuccessful when Katherine assured the King that she always deferred to his wisdom in theological matters.

Other historians, however, discount the role of factions under Henry. At the most extreme end, George Bernard questions their very existence and describes Henry as a monarch wholly in control of policy. Lucy Wooding accepts the existence of factions but denies that Henry was open to manipulation and a victim of factional intrigue. In her view, "Henry had strong opinions and he shaped and pursued his policies with confidence and authority". It was Henry who made and broke factions, not factions which made use of Henry.*

There is some truth in this, but the King was not as all-controlling as Wooding suggests. Other people fed him ideas, played on his prejudices, and influenced his judgements. Henry's unpredictability, impatience with failure, desire for quick solutions, and vulnerability to flattery – not to mention attractive women – made him susceptible to manipulation at moments of stress. So there were times when the King could impose his will on individuals and factions, and other times when he could be persuaded by them.

There has also been controversy about the role

* See footnote on p. 21. For Wooding, *Henry VIII* (London, 2008).

of factions under Edward and Mary. The conventional account was that the mid-Tudor court and council were factional battlegrounds, causing strife that was part of the so-called "mid Tudor crisis". Supposedly, during Edward's minority, the nobility was fighting for control of the regime, and under Mary conciliar divisions paralysed the government.

Modern historians are not convinced. They think Protector Somerset's fall from power under Edward was the result of his misgovernance, *not* of factional intrigue. A united front of councillors – not a rival faction – ranged against him in October 1549. There is also a consensus that after Somerset's dismissal the Edwardian council governed effectively, introducing reforms and making peace with France. Yet it is hard to deny either the existence of factions or that the reign was marked by a series of coups (both successful and failed), purges and conspiracies, far more of them than at any other time in the 16th century.

What of Mary's council? This is now thought to have been remarkably cohesive and efficient. Although large, it was successful in executing royal policy, whether negotiating Mary's marriage treaty in England's interests, ending the schism with Rome, or kick-starting reforms to restore the coinage (after earlier debasements). Of course there were disagreements, even individual rivalries – between Stephen Gardiner and William Lord Paget, for instance – but Mary rarely let them get out of hand. Consequently, there was no dramatic fall of ministers or intimates, as occurred under Henry VIII and Edward VI. Even after the disastrous loss of Calais in January 1558, the government held together.

The extent of factional conflict under Elizabeth has been reappraised, too. More than 50 years ago, Conyers Read and Sir John Neale both contended that Elizabethan politics were factional in character. During the 1560s Leicester, and Cecil were said to be enemies; after 1572, factional conflict arose between Cecil, now Lord Burghley, and Walsingham; and then in the 1590s, the rivalry between Sir Robert Cecil and Robert, second Earl of Essex, culminated in the 1601 Essex rising.

The historian Simon Adams rejects this interpretation, arguing that persistent factionalism *only* emerged in the closing decade of the reign when the aging Elizabeth lost her grip on politics and the rising star Essex would brook no rival.[*] Janet Dickinson goes even further. She thinks that even in the closing decade there was no real evidence of factionalism; previous historians, she insists, have underestimated how successfully the two Cecils (Lord Burghley and his son Robert) worked with Essex.[**]

So where does the truth lie? Adams is undoubt-

---

[*] Simon Adams, *Leicester and the Court: Essays on Elizabethan Politics* (Manchester, 2002).
[**] Janet Dickinson, *Court Politics and the Earl of Essex, 1589-1601* (London, 2011).

edly right in dismissing the notion that Elizabethan political life was polarised into factions *before* the 1590s. The Elizabethan elite was so interconnected by ties of blood and marriage that few political relationships could be exclusive. Furthermore, there were many routes to Elizabeth's favour: she listened to political counsel and private suits from diverse councillors and courtiers, including the women of the privy chamber. Unsurprisingly, then, each courtier turned to a range of patrons – not just one – to advance his or her interests or promote particular policies.

Yet Adams's picture of Elizabethan political life as essentially consensual is not persuasive. Certainly, there were issues over which leading men (and women) were united, often in opposition to the Queen. Almost everyone, for example, supported Mary of Scotland's exclusion from the succession in the 1570s and her eventual execution. But it is also clear that some of Elizabeth's councillors and courtiers heartily disliked each other. The Earl of Sussex, for example, loathed Leicester, and Essex could not abide Sir Walter Raleigh. More importantly, councillors often disagreed about important questions of policy, such as the wisdom of intervening in the religious wars abroad, whether or not Elizabeth should marry a Catholic, and whether religious conformity should be imposed on Protestants.

For the most part, these disagreements did not prevent Elizabethans from co-operating cordially in council or at court. They shared a strong sense of public duty and responsibility, partly derived from their humanist backgrounds, and they also felt the need to pull together in the face of the Catholic threat. Besides, Elizabeth frowned upon in-fighting between courtiers. She herself was intensely loyal – even forbearing – towards her intimates, and the chances of a whispering campaign against one of them being successful was extremely low. So political casualties were rare. Norfolk was the only privy councillor to lose his head before 1601, and there were very few dismissals from household positions or the council.

Nonetheless, it is hard to share the rosy view that Elizabeth's last decade was free from bitter factional disputes. It is true that Cecil and Burghley worked hard to keep the peace. But Essex became a magnet for men disaffected with the regime because of its policies, Elizabeth's failure to distribute patronage more widely, and what they saw as the *regnum Cecilium* (the dominance of the Cecils). The Earl was seen as the man who would challenge the younger Cecil and other political "enemies" such as Raleigh.

After Burghley's death in 1598, Essex's ambition to become Elizabeth's principal councillor and his hostility to Robert Cecil's peace policy towards Spain raised political tension alarmingly. Convinced that his enemies were plotting against him, Essex acted erratically while lord lieutenant in Ireland, and on returning to court was punished with the loss of his offices. Financially ruined when Elizabeth would not renew a lucrative royal grant, Essex mounted an abortive rising in London on 8 February 1601. He and some 300 followers – mainly knights and some noblemen – took to the streets of London, declaring that they were acting to save the state from Cecil and his friends, evil councillors who, he said, were conspiring to enthrone the Spanish Infanta on Elizabeth's death. Essex's expectation that the City would support him proved illusory, and the rising collapsed within a day. Nonetheless, it was a shocking event.

Essex's execution brought factional conflict to an end. After it Elizabeth broadened the political elite somewhat by adding four men to the privy council, including two noblemen, and over the next two years, the regime was stable. During Elizabeth's last illness all her privy councillors and nobles worked together to ensure James VI's smooth accession.

Was there a Tudor despotism?

Educated people in Tudor times thought they lived in a "mixed monarchy", a state in which the monarch governed with a council and parliament under the rule of law. Historians today think that on the whole they were right. Some even speak of a "monarchical republic", a state ruled by a prince but in which the "better sort" of people participated in government at the national and local level.

The term "monarchical republic" is problematic, but it is true that a relatively wide group of officeholders – not a narrow clique – worked voluntarily to make and implement national laws and local orders. Without a paid bureaucracy, police force or standing army, the active co-operation of these men was vital for governance, and their support was secured by persuasion, patronage, negotiation and propaganda. Although the Reformation fractured national unity, Henry VIII and his children usually proved able to convince their subjects that ruler and ruled shared similar humanist and Christian values and interests. This kind of state can hardly be styled a despotism.

Yet, at the same time the Tudor state was often oppressive, relying upon violence and coercion to impose its will. As we have seen, Henry VII used bonds and recognizances against members of the nobility and gentry, and had few scruples about disinheriting lawful heirs. Both he and his son used acts of attainder or instigated show trials to rid themselves of suspected traitors. In just one year (1495) seven important figures were indicted and executed, including the King's Chamberlain, King's Steward, Clerk of the Jewels and Dean of St Paul's. Altogether, during Henry VIII's reign, the axe fell on around two dozen prominent figures either by act of attainder (as in Cromwell's case) or after trials where the verdict was preordained (as with Sir Thomas More, John Fisher and Anne Boleyn).

When Henry VIII extended the scope of the

treason laws to include "treason by words", any verbal or written critique of his policies, especially the royal supremacy, became extremely risky. Between 1532 and 1540, 294 people were accused of treason by words, 63 of whom were executed. Henry's successors also broadened the scope of the treason laws by extending them to religious dissidents. Mary famously used heresy laws to burn Protestants; less well known is an Act of 1555 that made it treason to speak against the return to Rome. Elizabeth's 1585 statute against Jesuits condemned 123 Catholics to death on charges of treason.

Equally, the Tudor response to rebellion was for the most part pitiless. Violence marked the suppression of all rebellions: around a thousand people probably died at the Battle of Blackheath in 1497 when Henry VII defeated the West Country rebels, while Dussindale in 1549 became the graveyard of between one and two thousand of the Norfolk rebels.

Reprisals were usually severe for the survivors. More than 170 were hanged for their part in the northern risings of 1536-37 under Henry VIII; the Earl of Warwick and Lord Russell executed hundreds after the 1549 risings in Edward's reign; Mary agreed to the executions of around fifty rebels after Wyatt's Rebellion of 1554; and at least 600 of the "meaner sort" were executed for their part in the 1569 Northern Rising under Elizabeth, about ten per cent of the total rebel force. Rebels had no recourse to trial, and their bodies (drawn and quartered after the hangings) were displayed prominently in market towns both to deter others and to demonstrate state power. By contrast, Henry VII preferred exacting heavy fines rather than ordering executions.

Out of fear of rebellion, the government and local magistrates also came down hard on anyone heard criticising their social superiors, spreading seditious rumours, or voicing dangerous opinions. The Tudor state could be equally oppressive in its use of the criminal code. Difficult economic conditions, fear of disorder, moral imperatives, and a concern for conformity, all drove an expansion in the number of criminal statutes dealing with matters such as witchcraft, prophesy, vagrancy and sodomy.

Despite extensive use of pardons, the number of men and women executed for a felony was extraordinarily high. According to one estimate, there may have been as many as 75,000 judicial hangings between the years 1530 and 1630, a figure greater than at any subsequent time. Those found guilty of misdemeanours – such as pilfering, begging, prostitution and scolding – could also be punished severely, being whipped, pilloried, even branded.

So, while not a despotism, the Tudor regime was unquestionably authoritarian and could be tyrannical towards anyone who did not conform to the requirements or standards set by governments.

Why were there so many rebellions in England between 1536 and 1570?

Each Tudor monarch faced at least one major revolt and many riots. But during the years from 1536 to 1570 there was an unusual cluster of armed risings. The main participants in those of 1536 and 1549 were members of the "commons", although gentlemen also became involved. The risings of 1537 and 1554 were the brainchild of gentlemen, while noblemen instigated the northern risings of 1569-70. All social groups, therefore, and most regions of England came out in armed protest at one time or another during these decades.

The leaders of the 1536 risings under Henry VIII which began in Yorkshire did not consider themselves rebels. They proclaimed that they were participating in a "pilgrimage" to petition the King "for the reformation of that which is amiss within this realm and for the punishment of heretics and subverters of the laws". The "reformation" they sought included the re-establishment of dissolved monasteries, an end to novel taxes, and some agrarian reforms, such as a return to reasonable entry fines (payment upon entering a tenancy). As Ethan Shagan puts it:

> the pilgrims strove for a legitimate voice with which to oppose a regime whose radical fiscal and

Opposite: Portrait of Mary I (1516 - 1558) by Antonis Mor

ecclesiastical policies had severely depleted its stockpile of goodwill and instinctive obedience.*

The majority of the pilgrims did not aim to overthrow the regime, and after the King's representative promised a parliament to consider their grievances, the 50,000 or so men in arms agreed to go home. Henry VIII naturally saw it differently and branded them all rebels.

The East Anglian rebels of 1549 likewise petitioned the government to redress their grievances, although the target of their anger was not Edward's regime. Those who camped on Mousehold Heath and elsewhere supported Somerset's policy of restricting enclosure and

* Ethan Shagan, *Popular Politics and the English Reformation* (Cambridge, 2003).

MID-TUDOR RISINGS

1536 Lincolnshire Rising (Oct). Risings in six northern counties, called the Pilgrimage of Grace. At its height perhaps some 50,000 took part (Oct-Dec).
1537 Sir Francis Bigod's rising in East Yorkshire (Jan).
1548 Rising at Helston (Cornwall), culminating in the murder of William Body.
1549 "Popular commotions" in more than 25 counties of lowland England (spring and summer). The Western Rising in Cornwall, Devon and Somerset (June-Aug). The Norfolk rising (July-Aug).
1554 Wyatt's Rebellion (Jan).
1569 The Northern Rebellion (Oct-Dec).
1570 Leonard Dacre's rising in Yorkshire (Jan). ■

seemed to sympathise with Cranmer's religious reforms. Their grievances were directed against the local gentry whose agrarian practices – such as running rabbits over tenants' land, over-grazing the commons with huge flocks of sheep, and enclosing pieces of common land for private use – caused deep resentment.

The Mousehold leaders (mainly wealthier tenants) took a legalistic course in petitioning the government and bringing the gentry to book under a tree on the heath, what they called "a tree of reformation". But their protest escalated into rebellion when the government ordered them to disperse. Then the more radical smallholders and landless pushed the leaders to reject the pardons offered and assault Norwich. (The rebels were eventually defeated by an army led by the Earl of Warwick.)

Unlike the East Anglian protesters, the Western rebels demanded radical changes to government policy: a return to orthodox religion as stated in the Six Articles of 1539, the reinstatement of the traditional Latin Mass, and the removal of a new tax on sheep and cloth. Another contrast is that the men from Cornwall acted as rebels from the very start. Rather than negotiate, they captured St Michael's Mount, marched into Devon, occupied Plymouth, and on 2 July besieged Exeter for six weeks. Indeed, they seemed even more aggressive than their Devonshire allies who were prepared to negotiate with the gentry and set up a camp outside Exeter while the siege was on.

Nonetheless, the risings in the East and West had some similar features. First, they did not come out of the blue but were preceded by riots or disturbances in nearby areas. Trouble in Cornwall began with the murder of an archdeacon, William Body, in April 1548 when he was trying to impose the Edwardian injunction against idolatry. In East Anglia trouble brewed in Yarmouth in 1548, and during May the next year there were enclosure riots in Suffolk.

Second, local government in both areas was weak. There was no strong aristocratic presence in the South West after Henry VIII destroyed the Courtenay family, nor in East Anglia because of the imprisonment of Norfolk. The local gentry in both areas had little credibility, and in some cases were hated. As a result, the "commotions" starting in both places escalated into regional risings.

Third, the initial protesters in Cornwall and East Anglia were probably inspired to act by reports of disorder and governmental offers of pardon in other parts of the country. News travelled fast by word of mouth. The "commotions" in 1549 extended well beyond East Anglia and the South West. Camps were set up Hampshire, Essex, Oxfordshire, Cambridgeshire and Hertfordshire, from where petitions were sent to the government. Many risings were contained, but in some places, such as Oxfordshire, they had to be suppressed by force. Edward's government was taken by storm; unsurprisingly it could not cope and disorder snowballed.

The 1554 rebellion against Queen Mary, led by Sir Thomas Wyatt in Kent, was quite different. It was planned at court in late 1553. The conspirators – nobles and leading members of the gentry – originally devised a four-pronged regional rising against Mary which was aimed at stopping her marriage to Philip of Spain. In his propaganda, Wyatt concentrated on the marriage, a popular cause, but it was anti-Catholic feeling which motivated many of the participants. The original conspirators were all Protestants, and Maidstone – a main recruiting ground for the rebels – was a strong Protestant centre. As Kent had been badly affected by the recent slump in the textile industry, a small number of unemployed may have joined Wyatt's ranks for economic reasons, although their grievances were never stated.

Had the rebellion been successful – and it very nearly was – Mary would surely have been deposed. Wyatt privately admitted his intention was to put Elizabeth, married to an English nobleman, on the throne in her half-sister's place. But, at his trial, he strongly denied she was involved in his plot.

Fifteen years later, in October 1569, Elizabeth herself faced a serious rebellion (the Northern Rebellion) which would have also, had it been successful, resulted in the deposition of the monarch. The Earls of Northumberland and Westmorland wanted the Pope to excommunicate Elizabeth. This, they thought, would justify their armed rebellion and her later deposition. But the Pope delayed acting, and the two men had to maintain the fiction that they were loyal to Elizabeth and simply protesting against misgovernance. In their first proclamation they announced that they were raising arms to remove evil councillors, protect the true Catholic faith, and restore the ancient nobility. Not wanting to put Mary of Scotland's life in danger, they did not call her the rightful queen but merely declared – in their second proclamation – their intention to "make known" Elizabeth's rightful successor.

The motives behind their drastic actions were complex. Religion was important but so was the erosion of their power in the North under the Protestant Queen: Northumberland had lost his prestigious post as Warden of the Borders; Westmorland was in debt. The Earls were also reacting to fears that Elizabeth was planning to put them under arrest.

It used to be argued that their followers were their tenants and retainers who backed them out of feudal loyalty, but roughly 80 percent of the known rebels had no feudal link to the Earls. Krista Kesselring, moreover, argues convincingly that the majority of the rebels – some 6,000 men – willingly took up arms because of their dissatisfaction with the religious changes.[*] The rebels marched or rode under banners depicting the five wounds of Christ,

---

[*] K. J. Kesselring, *The Northern Rebellion of 1569: Faith, Politics, and Protest in Elizabethan England* (Basingstoke, 2007).

hung large crucifixes around their necks, and wore red crosses. When they entered Durham and Ripon Cathedrals, they destroyed English Prayer Books and held a Catholic Mass.

After 1570, there were no major rebellions. Why was this? The agrarian grievances of the poor had not disappeared, nor was religion any less divisive. During the 1580s and 1590s, scarcity of food, unemployment and the burdens of war created hardship that could easily have escalated into risings. Indeed, between 1581 and 1602, London witnessed 35 significant riots, while in the mid 1590s food riots occurred in Essex, Kent, Somerset and elsewhere. But these "commotions" were all contained before they spiralled into rebellion.

We can only speculate about the reasons for this relative quietude. One possibility is that during the war against Spain the government's decision to avoid new forms of taxation, its care to explain military demands, and its calls for national solidarity prevented widespread protests against misgovernance.

We can also surmise that the commons could no longer attract leadership from the "better sort" as they had in earlier risings. Social changes were drawing the yeomanry closer to the gentry in their material interests and cultural attitudes; their education and rising prosperity made them all too aware of the dangers to the social hierarchy to consider taking the lead in social protest.

How did the Tudors deal with Ireland?

Before 1541, Ireland was a lordship of the English crown, not a separate kingdom. The monarch had direct control only over the English Pale (five small counties around Dublin), which was governed by a lord deputy who was usually a Fitzgerald earl of Kildare. Outside the Pale were two geo-political areas: a central zone run by the great Anglo-Irish families (including the Fitzgeralds, who were also known as the Geraldines); and the western and northern parts containing Gaelic lordships following Irish (Brehon) law and custom.

Ireland posed security problems for the early Tudors: how to protect the Pale from Gaelic raids; how to prevent Anglo-Irish nobles from supporting a pretender, as when Kildare recognised Lambert Simnel; and how to stop foreign powers exploiting disaffection within the island.

Until the Geraldine revolt of 1534, the early Tudors relied on the Earl of Kildare's network of connections and alliances to maintain royal authority outside the Pale. The revolt – provoked by the crown when it attempted to reduce Geraldine power – changed all that. Sensitive to a rebellion just when he was embarking on the break with Rome, Henry VIII sent a huge army to crush the rising and ordered the execution of six senior Geraldines. But without their influence, the political situation in Ireland became dangerously unstable, an instability which led to unrest, rebellion and war.

Deciding he needed direct control, Henry had himself declared "King" instead of "Lord" of Ireland in the Irish parliament of 1541. All inhabitants – Gaelic as well as Anglo-Irish – were now his subjects under English law. Accompanying this constitutional change was a new policy, known as "surrender and regrant", a process whereby Gaelic chieftains had to submit to the King and in return would enter the English peerage before being given back (or having "regranted") their lands by royal title. When making their submissions, the lords were required to accept Henry as Supreme Head of the Church of Ireland.

The historians Brendan Bradshaw and Christopher Maginn both view "surrender and regrant" as a conciliatory policy, aimed at integrating Ireland peacefully into the Tudor state.[*] They are probably right; although the Irish were now expected to adopt English customs and language, a cross-section of Irish society approved the policy. As for Henry, he preferred it to further military efforts; reform would be cheaper and not distract him from war on the continent.

Tudor governments, however, soon lost confidence in reform because it did not deliver the stability the crown demanded. There was unrest in Ulster because English primogeniture conflicted

---

[*] Brendan Bradshaw, *The Irish Constitutional Revolution of the Sixteenth Century* (Cambridge, 2008); Christopher Maginn, '"Surrender and Regrant" in the Historiography of Sixteenth-Century Ireland', *The Sixteenth Century Journal*, 38 (2007), pp. 955-74.

with the Gaelic system (known as tanistry) for passing on the leadership of a clan. Under tanistry, the heir apparent or tanist (not necessarily the eldest son) was elected while the chief was still alive. Moreover, Scottish migration into Ulster raised security concerns because it was believed, though quite wrongly, that the Scots were agents of the French crown.

As a result, from the late 1540s Tudor governments lurched towards military solutions. Between 1546 and 1603 there was not a single year when government forces were not engaged in military operations in some part of Ireland, with each war waged bigger than the previous one and affecting ever wider areas of the country.

Combining conciliation with coercion, English governments now devised a plantation policy, under which English colonists or "planters" were settled on lands previously occupied by Gaelic clans. The first plantation began in 1556 in Laois and Offaly (renamed Queen's and King's counties). Two-thirds of midland Leinster was confiscated from the warring O'Mores, O'Connors and O'Demseys, who were replaced with settlers of proven loyalty. As well making the Pale less vulnerable, the plantation policy was supposed to encourage neighbouring Gaelic communities to adopt English laws and culture. What it actually did was ensure 50 years of border warfare.

During the 1560s and early 1570s plans were advanced for a similar settlement of land in Ulster and Munster. The objective now was also to spread Protestantism. The schemes of private adventurers to establish plantations in Ulster failed, but not before 600 Scots (mostly women and children) were massacred on Rathlin Island in 1575. In Munster, however, the government successfully settled Protestant Englishmen on the lands confiscated after the violent suppression of a Catholic rebellion led by the Earl of Desmond (1579-83).

Vincent Carey is one of a number of historians who argue that the English regime was by this time, if not earlier, bent on conquest, colonisation, even genocide.[*] The Queen and her advisers, Carey contends, saw the Irish as savages and employed terror tactics against them. Elizabeth may have been more disposed to conciliation to save money and prevent an escalation of unrest, but her senior officials in Ireland thought this "feminine" and weak.

Some historians, however, don't share Carey's view. They argue that conciliation was not abandoned until the 1590s, and that the violence the crown showed towards the Irish was no different

---

[*] Vincent Carey, 'Elizabeth I and State Terror in Sixteenth Century Ireland', in Donald Stump, Linda Shenk and Carole Levin (eds), *Elizabeth I and the 'Sovereign Arts': Essays in Literature, History, and Culture* (Tempe, AZ, 2011); David Edwards, Padraig Lenihan and Clodagh Tait (eds), *Age of Atrocity: Violence and Political Conflict in Early Modern Ireland* (Dublin, 2007).

in kind from that doled out to rebels in England.[*] The English, says Brendan Kane, did not think of Ireland as an overseas colony inhabited by an inferior race of savages but as a crown territory whose Catholic population was endangering and disturbing the realm. Malcolm Smuts agrees:

> Tudor humanists believed that to serve the public good they needed to suppress public enemies, reforming them if possible but destroying them if reformation proved unavailing.

No one, though, disputes that conciliation died with the rising led by Hugh O'Neill, Earl of Tyrone, also known as the Nine Years' War (1594-1603). This was the most extensive and long-lasting of the Tudor rebellions in Ireland, spreading throughout Ulster, Munster and Connaught, involving other Gaelic chieftains and attracting support from Spain. Elizabeth spent some £2 million and mustered tens of thousands of conscript troops to force O'Neill's surrender.

After the eventual English victory at Kinsale in December 1601, the Queen endorsed a scorched earth campaign unprecedented in its scale and ferocity. This, she felt, was justified because of O'Neill's treason, the humiliation he had inflicted on her armies, the devastation his allies had caused

---

[*] Brendan Kane, 'Ordinary Violence? Ireland as Emergency in the Tudor State', and Malcolm Smuts, 'Organized Violence in the Elizabethan Monarchical Republic', *History*, 99 (2014).

in Munster, and his successful summoning of Spanish aid. But the result of her Lord Deputy's reprisals was famine and misery. Elizabeth's policy in Ireland was a disastrous failure.

Foreign relations

How did England's relations with France change during the 16th century?

It is customary to think of France as England's main enemy during the first half of the 16th century, and then as a reluctant friend because of Elizabeth's worsening relationship with Philip II of Spain. The actual picture, however, is more complex.

On his accession, Henry VIII was not immediately bent on renewing the Hundred Years' War against France. Although attracted to the chivalric ideal of winning honour in battle, he listened to his father's advisers who were counselling peace. It was two years before he went to war. Then he was encouraged to do so by younger nobles at court and diplomatic representations from the "Holy League" (an alliance formed against Louis XII of France in October 1511).

Henry told parliament that his war was a crusade in defence of the papacy, but he also hoped to equal the military achievements of Edward III and Henry

V by reconquering the territories held by his ancestors and in asserting his claim to the French throne. In March 1512 Pope Julius II secretly recognised Henry's claim and even talked privately of crowning him in Paris. Henry's dynastic and personal ambitions therefore meshed well with his religious fervour.

The first English campaign of 1512 was in Gascony (one of the former Plantagenet possessions) and was disastrous, mainly due to the failings of the English army command. Henry's second foray on the continent was successful, his army winning the notable, if small, Battle of the Spurs and taking possession of Tournai and Thérouanne.

The accession of Francis I in 1515 added a new dimension to Henry's relations with France. The two kings became personal rivals, competing in diplomatic displays, the exchange of extravagant gifts and the magnificence of their courts. They briefly went to war in 1523, when the Duke of Suffolk, marched on Paris – another ignominious failure – but otherwise, until July 1543, they somewhat surprisingly spent most of their reigns at peace with one other.

Indeed Henry won himself a reputation as the peace-maker of Europe after Wolsey negotiated the Treaty of London in 1518, and the King displayed a flamboyant friendship with Francis at the Field of Cloth of Gold in 1520. In 1527 and 1532, the two monarchs signed treaties of alliance. Although Francis seemed ready to launch a crusade against

Henry in 1538 as the ally of the Holy Roman Emperor, Charles V, the threat never materialised.

Henry's preference for peace during these years owed much to his circumstances at home: he was preoccupied with the annulment and break with Rome, faced domestic unrest and, anyway, had insufficient funds for new wars. None of these conditions applied in the early 1540s. For some historians, their absence is sufficient to explain Henry's new campaign against France but David Potter argues he chose war for *strategic* not chivalric reasons.[*] Were he to remain neutral in a renewal of conflict between Francis and the Holy Roman Emperor, Charles V, he would be without a European ally and face international isolation, even ostracism, when the two rulers ultimately came to terms. It was not immediately apparent which side Henry would take, but he eventually chose Charles as his ally in summer 1542, mainly because the Emperor had greater military power.

Henry's last war in France was different from his earlier campaigns. His objective was to annex any territory he could rather than conquer ex-Plantagenet lands or assume the crown of France, hence his decision to besiege Boulogne in 1544. He had no claim to the city, and his war against it was more destructive and expensive than all his earlier efforts, with far-reaching financial implications: the debasement of the currency, the

---

[*] David Potter, *Henry VIII and Francis I: The Final Conflict* (Leiden, 2011).

sale of ex-monastic lands, and the partial dissolution of the chantries. The capture and maintenance of Boulogne cost £3,501,453 until it was sold back to France by treaty in 1550.

The King's final war against France also adversely affected his relationship with Scotland. In 1513 James IV had invaded England as Louis XII's ally, so in the early 1540s Henry feared that James V would dance to the French tune, especially as he had taken Mary of Guise as his wife. In 1542, therefore, before embarking on his continental campaign, Henry ordered troops into Scotland. Military success was immediate at Solway Moss but this turned out to be a pyrrhic victory. Henry's browbeating efforts to force the Scots into accepting a marriage between his son and their new queen, the infant Mary, escalated into warfare, known as the "Rough Wooing", which brought in French troops in 1547. The much-needed peace of 1550 left Scotland as a virtual protectorate of France and a security risk to England.

Had Mary I not married a Habsburg prince, peace would probably have continued between England and France when she came to the throne. As it was, the French King, Henry II, offered support to Wyatt in his rising against the marriage, provided asylum for English rebels and conspirators, and sent 3,000 troops to Scotland. These provocations encouraged Mary to join her Spanish husband, Philip II, in his war against France. The immediate *casus belli* was an English émigré's raid on

Elizabeth I (1533 - 1603), the Armada Portrait

Scarborough Castle on 28 April 1557. This was believed to have been orchestrated or at least backed by the French King.

Although English troops helped the Spanish win at St Quentin, Mary was humiliated in January 1558 when a French army under the Duke of Guise captured Calais in a brilliant mid-winter attack. This meant that Elizabeth came to the throne when England's relations with France were at their nadir. She quickly patched up a peace at Cateau-Cambrésis in April 1559, but Calais stayed in French hands, Scotland remained a French puppet state, and Henry II supported his daughter-in-law Mary's claim to the English throne.

Henry II's death in July 1559, however, changed everything. Internal conflict quickly crippled France, and Scotland slipped out of its control. Initially, the French were able to send troops to help quell a rebellion led by the Protestant Lords of the Congregation, but after Elizabeth dispatched an army to assist the rebels in February 1560 the government in Paris had to agree to the evacuation of all foreign soldiers from Scotland. France's hold on the northern British kingdom was over. Safe from French intervention, the Scottish parliament introduced a Protestant Reformation in August 1560.

Mary Queen of Scots's return to her native land in August 1561 re-awakened fears in England that the "auld alliance" between France and Scotland would be renewed. In reality, Mary wanted an entente with England in order to safeguard her place in the succession and had no immediate ambitions to return Scotland to Rome. Mary's kin, the powerful Guise family, was moreover far too preoccupied with political and religious problems in France to get involved directly in Scotland.

After Mary's deposition and flight to England, Charles IX of France demanded her reinstatement and immediate release from captivity. For several years, Elizabeth did try – albeit unsuccessfully – to negotiate Mary's restoration on terms that would be in England's interests. But at the same time she gave military and diplomatic support to the Scottish Protestant lords in the civil war that had engulfed

Scotland after Mary's overthrow. Eventually, in April 1572, the French King abandoned his role as Mary's protector when he signed the Anglo-French Treaty of Blois. Elizabeth then stepped up her aid to the Scottish Protestants, helping them gain power and impose order in the name of James VI.

It was only after James reached adulthood in 1579 that a renewal of the "auld alliance" again became a threat. In a bid for independence, the Scottish King broke with his Anglophile councillors and turned to his French cousin Esmé Stuart, whom he created Duke of Lennox. For several years English policy stumbled in response to this crisis, but in the end James and Elizabeth struck a deal. Under the 1586 Treaty of Berwick, James became a pensioner of the English Queen.

The French had been unable to profit from the instability in Scotland because of the religious wars in their own realm. These wars had a huge impact on England's relationship with France from 1562 until 1598, the year when Henry IV signed a long-lasting religious peace (the Edict of Nantes) and secured his hold on the French throne. In the long period of warfare before this, Elizabeth consistently gave aid to her co-religionists, the Huguenots, in their struggles against the French crown and Catholic Guise family. Her motives were both religious and strategic; it is pointless to debate which of the two was more important.

In 1562, English aid was open: Elizabeth signed a treaty with Huguenot leaders and sent troops to

Le Havre in Normandy. Her reward was supposed to be the return of Calais. But the English intervention was catastrophic since the French Regent sent both Catholic and Huguenot troops to reclaim Le Havre. After this Elizabeth never fully trusted the Huguenots again even though she continued to assist them, albeit discreetly and indirectly. She allowed military supplies and soldiers to reach Huguenot strongholds and granted Protestant refugees a safe haven in English territories. In 1568, £4,000 was transported covertly from the Tower of London to La Rochelle.

At the same time, Elizabeth was determined to avoid a rupture with France's Catholic King, whose friendship she needed once England's relations with Spain began to deteriorate. For this reason, she maintained the defensive Treaty of Blois after the terrible massacres of Huguenots that began on St Bartholomew's Eve, 1572, in Paris and other French cities. Elizabeth's desultory marriage negotiations with Francis, Duke of Alençon (later Anjou), between 1572 and 1576 were intended to serve the same purpose. In 1581, when war against Spain looked imminent, she tried – unsuccessfully – to negotiate an offensive alliance with Henry III.

Only during the war against Spain in the late 1580s did Elizabeth again aid the Huguenots openly. The Protestant Henry of Navarre had succeeded to the French throne as Henry IV, but the Catholic League, supported by Spain, refused to recognise his right to be king. Already at war against Spain,

Elizabeth sent him men and money (as loans) in their common cause.

Their alliance survived Henry IV's conversion to Catholicism in 1593, but Elizabeth felt angry and betrayed when the King made a separate peace with Spain in 1598. Their relationship soured further as she demanded repayment of debts and he remonstrated against English privateering. By the end of the reign, the two monarchs were uneasy friends, with few shared interests and many points of tension.

Why did England go to war against Spain in 1585?

War against Spain was not inevitable. Admittedly, most Elizabethan Protestants feared and hated the Catholic Philip II, and a martial maritime group with powerful patrons at court wanted to break through the Spanish monopoly in the Americas. But Elizabeth and councillors such as Cecil hoped to avoid war. Spain was too great a military power to be taken on lightly and, besides, there were advantages in peace.

Trade with the Netherlands (Philip II's possession) was vital to English interests before 1570, and commerce with the Iberian peninsula itself soon grew in importance. The Spanish Company, established in 1577, became England's largest trading company, and many merchants who were not members of it also traded with Spain. As far as

England's security was concerned, France was thought the more dangerous enemy, because of Mary of Scotland's connections with the powerful Guises. Spain's friendship, therefore, could not easily be sacrificed.

Nonetheless, Anglo-Spanish relations were difficult during the years of peace. In retaliation for English piracy in the Channel, the Regent of the Netherlands banned the import of English goods in 1563, using the plague as an excuse, and Philip extended the embargo to all his Spanish dominions. As a result, England began to look for commercial outlets elsewhere, and found a temporary if unsatisfactory market in Emden, a seaport in northwest Germany. In the end, the Regent relented and all trade was restored, but England was no longer quite so dependent on the Anglo-Antwerp axis. When Philip imposed a second embargo in January 1569, English merchants were ready to switch their main trading post to Hamburg.

Religious tensions, meanwhile, became increasingly serious. In 1566 Elizabeth's selection of a Protestant clergyman as ambassador to Spain ended badly when Philip dismissed him in March 1568 and the Queen appointed no successor. Shortly afterwards, Don Guerau de Spes, the Spanish ambassador to England since March 1568, began conspiring with English Catholics, continuing to do so until his dismissal at the end of 1571 for his role in the Ridolfi Plot. No replacement was appointed until late 1577.

It was, however, the Protestant revolt in the Netherlands that caused the greatest strain between the two rulers. Although in 1566 Elizabeth had not questioned Philip's right to suppress unrest in his own territories, his dispatch of a huge army to Brussels caused revulsion and alarm. The Queen and her council feared that Philip intended to invade England as soon as he had crushed the Protestants in the Netherlands.

The first crisis with Spain came in early 1569. Elizabeth had ordered Spanish treasure bound for the army in Brussels to be unloaded onto English shores the previous December. Whether or not she intended to confiscate the gold is uncertain, but the Spanish ambassador, De Spes, was convinced that this was indeed her purpose. His clumsy mishandling of the situation resulted in a trade embargo and a diplomatic cold war that lasted nearly five years.

At times during this period, Elizabeth and Philip were on the brink of actual war. Elizabeth's privateers launched regular attacks on Spanish shipping, and Philip came close to invading during 1570 and 1571. In 1572, after a new uprising in Holland and Zeeland, Elizabeth allowed English volunteers to fight alongside the rebels.

Elizabeth and Philip, however, repaired relations in 1574, and a new resident Spanish ambassador, Don Bernardino de Mendoza, arrived in England three years later. But the Netherlands remained a running sore. Philip rebuffed Elizabeth's offers of mediation in the conflict; Elizabeth, meanwhile, made diplomatic contact with William of Orange, the leader of the revolt. Although she would not send an army under Leicester's command to fight with him in Holland nor accept sovereignty of the rebellious provinces, as Orange wanted, she nonetheless lent £20,000 to the Protestant mercenary John, Count of the Palatinate, enabling him to raise an army to fight in support of the rebels in 1578. Elizabeth also sponsored Francis, Duke of Anjou, when he took up the Dutch cause. Between 1581 and 1582 she loaned him about £70,000, and in February 1582 he went to the Netherlands as her protégé, accompanied by a delegation of 40 or so English nobles and gentlemen.

To harass Spain further, Elizabeth agreed to Francis Drake's privateering voyage of December 1577 that ended with his circumnavigation of the globe. When Drake returned with ships full of Spanish booty, Elizabeth publicly knighted him and refused to return the treasure. Justifiably angered by these hostile acts, Philip sent troops to Smerwick in October 1580 to foment unrest in Ireland. He also permitted De Mendoza to enter into conspiracies to overthrow the Queen. After the ambassador's involvement in the Throckmorton Plot was discovered, Elizabeth expelled him from England. No new ambassador was appointed as a replacement.

In August 1585 Elizabeth concluded the Treaties of Nonsuch which committed her to sending an army to the Netherlands. By this time, she had little choice but to take direct action. The previous year Orange had been assassinated, leaving the rebels demoralised; Philip's general, Alexander, Prince of Parma, was brilliantly reconquering the rebellious provinces in the southern Netherlands and had begun to besiege Antwerp; and France's Henry III refused to take on his brother's mantle (and help the Dutch) after Anjou's death in 1584.

The Netherlands seemed doomed without English military assistance. Philip, moreover, had emerged as the leader of an international league against Protestantism, or so the English thought, for they learned in March 1585 that the King had signed the Treaty of Joinville with the Duke of Guise, the head of the French Catholic League. In May 1585, Philip's seizure of English shipping in Spanish ports convinced Elizabeth's council that he intended to use the vessels in an armada against England.

When Elizabeth signed the Treaties of Nonsuch and agreed to the dispatch of an army under Leicester to the Netherlands, she still had no desire for war against Spain. She hoped that her action would push Philip into a negotiated settlement. She did not declare war, but instead opened up at least five simultaneous sets of peace negotiations between 1585 and 1588; and she refused to assume sovereignty of the rebel Dutch provinces, now calling themselves the United Provinces. Philip, however, could hardly tolerate Drake's raids on the West Indies and Leicester's armed presence in the Netherlands. Besides, English and Dutch terms for a settlement were entirely unacceptable to him. Provoked into war, he launched the Grand Armada in 1588.

Throughout the war, Elizabeth's aims were limited: the destruction of the Spanish fleet so that it would pose no future threat to England; the security of the United Provinces; and the expulsion of Spanish troops from France. Some of her councillors were more ambitious: Essex, for example, wanted a knock-out blow against Spain. But Elizabeth prevailed. Even so, peace terms could not be reached. The armada was defeated, but Elizabeth's refusal to abandon the Dutch and Philip's aid to the Irish rebels prevented the formal cessation of hostilities in her lifetime.

Conclusion

On Elizabeth's death, her successor, James VI of Scotland, inherited all sorts of problems. The war had disrupted trade and caused widespread discontent; the royal finances were precarious; Ireland needed rebuilding; peace terms had to be agreed with Spain; Catholics were demanding toleration; Puritans were seeking reforms. It might seem from this that Elizabeth had failed badly as England's queen.

Yet these problems should not be exaggerated. As Janet Dickinson and Neil Younger argue, the 1590s were nothing like as nasty as is often maintained. These years, they rightly pronounce, "witnessed a government working at the peak of its capacity, dealing with serious problems with remarkable efficiency". Among its achievements was the successful generation of resources to fight a demanding war and the introduction of an innovative programme of legislation to contain the social problems brought on by four bad harvests in a row and a devastating plague.[*]

What is more, Elizabeth's war-time objectives were achieved. The Spanish threat to the United Provinces was lifted; Spanish forces left France; France's Henry IV was secure on his throne; Protestants in France were allowed a measure of toleration. At home, Elizabeth had imposed her Protestant settlement with considerable success, avoiding the religious upheavals experienced in Scotland, France and the Netherlands. Obviously, not all her subjects were satisfied with her rule, but when have governments ever experienced an absence of criticism and complaint? At news of the Queen's death and on the day of her funeral, there was an outpouring of grief which does not appear to have been stage-managed.

Like all the Tudors Elizabeth died naturally. Given that four monarchs from 1399 to 1485 had been deposed (five if we include one of the princes in the Tower) and two were to lose their thrones during the 17th century, this was no mean

---

[*] Janet Dickinson and Neil Younger, 'Just How Nasty Were the 1590s?', *History Today*, 64/7 (2014).

achievement and is a sign of the Tudors' political strength and acumen. They were all authoritarian, intelligent in the way they manipulated public opinion, and brilliant at using magnificence and propaganda to enhance royal power. Their legacy, therefore, was a stronger monarchy, a powerful state, and a transformed national Church.

GLOSSARY AND WHO'S WHO

Acts and Monuments: John Foxe's book, popularly known as "Foxe's Book of Martyrs". It came out in four editions under Elizabeth I and provided a history of the Roman Church's persecution of heretics, notably Lollards and Protestants.

Allen, William (1532–94): Catholic theologian and polemicist, who went into exile under Elizabeth I. He founded the English College at Douai in 1568, which became a training ground for priests on mission in England.

Auld Alliance: an alliance between France and Scotland that dated back to 1295 and was enacted to prevent England dominating the northern kingdom of Britain.

Babington Plot 1586: a plot involving the Catholic Anthony Babington. Its aim was to assassinate Elizabeth I and put the rescued Mary Queen of Scots on the English throne. Francis Walsingham used the plot to bring a charge of treason against Mary.

Bond of Association 1584: a bond entered into by Elizabeth I's subjects. They swore to hunt down perpetrators of an attempt on Elizabeth I's life and prevent any intended beneficiary of the assassination from inheriting the throne, even if he or she were completely innocent of the act. A modified version of the Bond was embodied in the 1585 Act for the Queen's Surety.

Cecil, Sir William (d. 1598): Elizabeth's principal

secretary from 1558 until 1572 and then Lord Treasurer till his death. He became Baron Burghley in 1571. He was the Queen's most influential councillor and leading manager of the realm.

Devereux, Robert, Earl of Essex (exec. 1601): the step-son of Leicester who became a prominent courtier and soldier during the war against Spain. He lost royal favour after failing to suppress rebellion in Ireland. In 1601 he was executed for treason.

Dudley, Robert, Earl of Leicester, (d.1588): Elizabeth's Master of the Horse who had hopes of marrying the Queen. He became a privy councillor in 1563 and was created Earl of Leicester in 1564.

Field of Cloth of Gold 1520: a summit held between Henry VIII and Francis I near Calais and lasting from 7 to 24 June 1520. It was noted for its magnificence.

Francis, Duke of Anjou (1555-84): the youngest son of King Henry II of France and brother of Francis II, Charles IX and Henry III. He was formerly the Duke of Alençon,

Hundred Years' War: the warfare waged from 1337 to 1453 between the English Plantagenet Kings and the Valois Kings of France. In dispute were English claims to the provinces of Aquitaine and Normandy and the French crown.

Justification by faith alone: the Protestant belief that salvation was attainable not by works (such as the Mass, confession, and pilgrimages) but simply by faith in Christ's redeeming sacrifice on the Cross. This faith was a gift from God.

Monopolies: patents issued by the monarch allowing monopolies over particular industries. They provided a source of revenue for the Crown and were a means of rewarding courtiers.

Predestination: the doctrine that God selected individuals for eternal life or death.

"Princes in the Tower": Edward V and Richard, Duke of York. two young sons of Edward IV and Elizabeth Woodville. Parliament declared that both princes – and their sister Elizabeth of York – were illegitimate. The princes disappeared in the Tower during 1483, probably murdered on the order of Richard III.

Treaty of London 1518: a pact, negotiated by Wolsey, that agreed to perpetual peace. It was signed in London by representatives from all the major powers and many lesser ones.

Walsingham, Sir Francis: Elizabeth I's principal secretary from December 1573 until his death in 1590.

FURTHER READING

In addition to the books in the footnotes:

Valuable Overviews of Aspects of the Tudors

Susan Brigden, *New Worlds, Lost Worlds: The Rule of the Tudors, 1485–1603* (London, 2000).

Susan Doran and Norman Jones (eds), *The Elizabethan World* (London, 2011).

Susan Doran, *England and Europe 1485-1603* (London, 1996).

Anthony Fletcher and Diarmaid MacCulloch, *Tudor Rebellions* (London, 1997).

S. J. Gunn, *Early Tudor Government, 1485-1558* (Basingstoke, 1995).

John Guy, The Tudors <www.tudors.org> AS/A2 Level.

Alec Ryrie, *The Age of Reformation: The Tudor and Stewart Realms, 1485-1603* (Harlow, 2009).

Robert Tittler and Norman Jones (eds), *A Companion to*

Tudor Britain. Blackwell Companions to British History (Oxford, 2004).

Andy Wood, *Riot, Rebellion and Popular Politics in Early Modern England* (Basingstoke, 2002).

Biographies and Political Studies

Sean Cunningham, *Henry VII* (London, 2007).

Thomas Penn, *Winter King: The Dawn of Tudor England* (London, 2011).

Lucy Wooding, *Henry VIII* (London, 2008).

Diarmaid MacCulloch, *The Boy King: Edward VI and the Protestant Reformation* (New York, 1999).

John Edwards, *Mary I: England's Catholic Queen* (New Haven, 2011).

Stephen Alford, *Burghley: William Cecil at the Court of Elizabeth I* (New Haven, 2008).

Susan Doran, *Elizabeth I and Her Circle* (Oxford, 2015).

⑇ CONNELL GUIDES

MORE IN OUR NEW HISTORY SERIES

Guides
The French Revolution
Winston Churchil
World War One
The Third Reich
Stalin
Lenin
Nelson
Napoleon
The Cold War
The American Civil War
The Normans
Russia and its Rulers
The Amerian Civil Rights Movement

Short Guides
Britain after World War Two
Edward VI
Mary I
The General Strike
The Suffragettes
President Truman
President Lincoln

"Connell Guides should be required reading in every school in the country."
Julian Fellowes, creator of Downton Abbey

"What Connell Guides do is bring immediacy and clarity: brevity with depth. They unlock the complex and offer students an entry route."
Colin Hall, Head of Holland Park School

"These guides are a godsend. I'm so glad I found them."
Jessica Enthoven, A Level student, St Mary's Calne

"Completely brilliant. I wish I were young again with these by my side. It's like being in a room with marvellous tutors. You can't really afford to be without them, and they are a joy to read."
Joanna Lumley

To buy any of these guides, or for more information, go to
www.connellguides.com
Or contact us on (020)79932644 / info@connellguides.com

LITERATURE GUIDES

Novels and poetry
Emma
Far From the Madding Crowd
Frankenstein
Great Expectations
Hard Times
Heart of Darkness
Jane Eyre
Lord of the Flies
Mansfield Park
Middlemarch
Mrs Dalloway
Paradise Lost
Persuasion
Pride and Prejudice
Tess of the D'Urbervilles
The Canterbury Tales
The Great Gatsby
The Poetry of Robert Browning
The Waste Land
To Kill A Mockingbird
Wuthering Heights

Shakespeare
A Midsummer Night's Dream
Antony and Cleopatra
Hamlet
Julius Caesar
King Lear
Macbeth
Othello
Romeo and Juliet
The Second Tetralogy
The Tempest
Twelfth Night

Modern texts
A Doll's House
A Room with a View
A Streetcar Named Desire
An Inspector Calls
Animal Farm
Atonement
Beloved
Birdsong
Hullabaloo
Never Let Me Go
Of Mice and Men
Rebecca
Spies
The Bloody Chamber
The Catcher in the Rye
The History Boys
The Road
Vernon God Little
Waiting for Godot

NEW
A Short History of English Literature
American literature
Dystopian literature
How to read a poem
How to read Shakespeare
The Gothic
The poetry of Christina Rossetti
Women in literature

INDEX

A
Act of Union of 1536 75–76
Acts and Monuments (Foxe) 59, 119
Adams, Simon 83–84
Allen, William 32, 119
Anglo-French Treaty of 1514 18
Anne, of Cleves, Queen 8, 26
Anne Boleyn, Queen 7–8, 10, 21, 23–26, *25*, 49, 80
Arthur, King (legend) 60
Arthur, Prince of Wales 14–16, 20, 22, 60
Attainders 14–15
Auld Alliance 108–109, 119

B
Babington Plot of 1586 33, 119
Beaufort, Margaret 6, 60
Bernard, George 23, 24, 43–44, 45, 47–48, 81
Bible 20, 38, 41, 47–48, 54
  English 41, 46, 48, 59
Black Death 36
Blackheath, Battle of 88
Blount, Elizabeth 19
Bond of Association of 1584 33, 119
Bonds 14–16
Bosworth Field, Battle of 6, 11, 12
Bucer, Martin 53

C
Calais 9, 83, 107, 110
Calvinism 43, 69
Canterbury, Archdiocese of 23–24, 44–45, 65–66
Catholics and Catholicism
  beliefs 42
  challenge to Elizabeth 30–34
  foreign policy 109–112, 115
  in Ireland 101–102
  legislation against 64–65, 88
  political factions 84–85
  Puritans and 70
  rebellions 95–97
  success issues and 28–29
  Treatise of Treasons, A 32
  see also Reformation
Cecil, William, 1st Baron Burghley 10, 31, 69–70, 83, 85, 119–120
Charles IX of France 108–109
Charles of Austria 36
Charles V of Spain, Holy Roman Emperor 21, 51–52, 105
Civil war 30, 34, 38–39, 79
"Classes" (secret gatherings) 71
Colet, John 38, 44
Collinson, Patrick 68, 79
Colonialism 100–102
Cranmer, Thomas 24, 26, 50–53, 58, 80–81
Cromwell, Thomas 24, 46–47, 49–50, 74, 80

D
Darnely, Henry Stuart, Lord 14, 33
Devereux, Robert, 2nd Earl of Essex 83–86, 120
"Devise", female succession 28–29
Dickens, A.G. 41
Dickinson, Janet 83, 116–117
Drake, Francis 114
Dudley, John 28, 51–52
Dudley, Robert, 1st Earl of Leicester 10, 17, 36, 69, 83–84, 114–115, 120

E
East Anglian riots 92–94
Edward III 7, 19
Edward IV 6, 11–13, 38–39, 72
Edward VI 8, 26–29, 61, *75*, 76, 82, 92–94
Edwardian Reformation 51–53
Elizabeth, of York 6–7, 11–12,

16, *17*
Elizabeth I 9–11, *107*
   factions under 84–86
   foreign policy 10–11, 101–103, 107–116
   health and exercise 61–62
   legacy 116–118
   parliaments 78–79
   rebellions under 95–96, 101–103
   religion under 58–59, 64–68, 96–97, 109
   right to reign 24–26, 28, 30–34, 55–56
   succession issues 34–40
   threats to rule 30–34, 68–70
Elton, Geoffrey 72, 74
England, life in 36–39
English Bible 41, 46, 48, 59
English Church 40–45, 48
Erasmus, Desiderius 21, 38, 47–48
Essex, Robert Devereux, 2nd Earl 83–86, 120
Evangelicals 42, 45, 50, 57, 81

F
Factions, political 80–86
Field of Cloth of Gold of 1520 104, 120
Foxe, John, *Acts and Monuments* 59, 119
France 9, 17–18, 22, 49, 103–111
   Calais, territory loss 9, 83, 107, 110
Francis, Duke of Anjou 36, 110, 114–115, 120
Francis I of France 21, 33, 104–105

G
Geraldine revolt 98
Government, innovations in 72–76
Grey, Frances 27
Grey, Jane, Lady 9, 28–30, 37
Grey, Katherine, Lady 35, 37, 39
Guise family 106, 108–109
Gunn, Steven 15, 16

H
Hebrew Bible 20, 38, 48
Henry II of France 20, 31, 61, 106–108
Henry VII 6–7, 11–18, *17*, 36, 38, 60, 72–74, 89
Henry VIII 7–8
   annulment 20–27
   children 10, 19–20, 24–26
   early reign 16–18, 60–61
   factions under 80–81
   foreign policy 103–106
   governmental changes 75–76
   images *17*, *63*
   later years 8, 61
   mistresses 19
   rebellions under 90, 98–99
   Reformation/break with Rome 20–27, 46–50
   regime 87–88
   succession issues 18–27
   will 34–35, 38, 47
Hornbooks 62
House of Commons 77–78
House of Lords 52, 56, 77
Huguenots 109–110
Humanism 37–38, 47–48
Hundred Years' War 103, 120

I
Ireland 12, 98–103, 114
Ives, Eric 23, 24, 28–29, 49, 80

J
James VI and I of Scotland and England 35, 38, 67–68, 109, 116
Jesuits 33, 59
Justification by faith alone 46, 49, 120

K

Katherine, of Aragon, Queen 7, 15, 19–22, 24
Katherine Howard, Queen 8, 26
Katherine Parr, Queen 8, 26, 81
Kesselring, Krista 96

L

Lake, Peter 69, 70
Lancaster, House of 6, 11–12
Landriano, Battle of 21
Latimer, Hugh 52
Leviticus (Bible) 20
Lollardy 41, 42
London 37, 62, 97
Louis XII of France 17, 106
Luther, Martin 21, 43
Lutherans 43, 52, 55, 64
    Justification by faith alone 46, 49, 120

M

Machiavelli, Niccolo 7
Margaret, Queen of Scots 27
Marian exiles 64, 69
Mary, Queen of France 27
Mary, Queen of Scots 33
    desposition 108–109
    execution 33, 84
    marriages 27, 33
    relationship with Elizabeth 10–11, 37, 108
    succession challenge 27, 31, 33–34, 37, 84
Mary I 9, 61, *90*
    Catholicism 9, 28–29, 53–54
    early years 20, 25
    government under 82–83
    rebellions under 95
    relations with France 106–107
    right to rule 28–30
Monasteries, dissolution of 45–46, 49, 77, 90
Monopolies 78–79, 121

N

Netherlands 111–115
"Nicodemites" 57

P

Parker, Matthew 65–66
Parliament 11, 33, 76–79
Pavia, Battle of 18
Penal laws against Catholics 64–65
Philip II of Spain 9, 32, 103, 106, 111–115
Pilgrimage of Grace 49
Plantagenet, House of 7, 15, 19
Plantation policy 100
Pole, Cardinal Reginald 18, 54
Pole, Edmund & Richard de la 16–18
Pope Clement VII 18, 20–22
Pope Julius II 104
Pope Pius V 31–32, 95–96
Prayer Books 52–53, 59, 64–65, 67
Predestination 64, 121
Presbyterianism 43, 66–67, 70–71
    Marprelate Tracts 71–72
"Princes in the Tower" 13, 121
Protestant Church 8, 28–31, 41, 50, 52–53
    Elizabethan era 10, 64–68, 100–101
    revolt in Netherlands 113–115
Protestants 33, 57
    beliefs 43
    burning of 9, 56, 58
Puritanism 43, 66–72, 78–79

R

Rebellions 83, 88–89, 90–97, 100–102
    in Netherlands 113–115
    timeline 92
Recognizances 14–16
Reformation

annulment of Henry VIII 20–27
confessional divisions 55
Edwardian 52–53
English church before 40–45
Monasteries, dissolution
    45–46, 49, 77, 90
parishioner response 56–59
process of 46–47, 108
reasons for 46–56
Religion, belief systems 42–43, 55
Rex, Richard 41, 48
Richard III 6, 12, 39, 73
Ridley, Nicholas 52
Ridolfi Plot 32, 112
Riots *see* Rebellions

S

Schools 62
Scotland 106–109
Separatists 67, 69
Seymour, Edward, 1st Earl of
    Hertford 35, 51
Seymour, Jane, Queen 8, *17*, 26
Shagan, Ethan 90–92
Shakespeare, William 11
Sidney, Mary, Lady 62
Simnel, Lambert 12, 98
Smuts, Malcolm 102
Somerset, Edward Seymour, 1st
    Duke 51, 82, 92
Spain 19, 97, 110–116
    Grand Armada 10–11, 33, 116
Starkey, David 23, 80
Stoke, battle of 12
Stuart, Arbella, Lady 38–39
Stuart, Esmé 109
Succession 28–30
    issues for Elizabeth I 34–40
    issues for Henry VIII 18–27
    legislation 25–26
Surrey, Howard Henry, Earl of 27

T

Theatre 62

Tower of London 10, 12–13, 15–16,
    27, 29, 30, 35, 110, 121
Treasons Act of 1571 32
Treaties of Nonsuch of 1585 114–115
Treaty of Berwick of 1586 109
Treaty of Blois of 1572 109–110
Treaty of Edinburgh of 1560 31
Treaty of London of 1518 104, 121
Tudors
    chronology of 13
    early challenges to 11–18
    factions and in-fighting 80–86
    family tree 4–5
    government innovations 72–76
    legacy 116–117
    life under 36–39
    state regime 86–89
    ten facts about 60–62
    use of name 7

V

Vermigli, Peter Martyr 53

W

Wales 14, 20, 60, 75
Walsingham, Francis 69–70, 121
Warbeck, Perkin 12–15
Wars of the Roses 6, 12
Whitehall Mural, The (van Leemput) *17*
Whitgift, John 67, 70
William I, Prince of Orange
    114–115
Wolsey, Thomas, Cardinal 21–23,
    45, 76, 80, 104
Wooding, Lucy 47–48, 81
Wyatt's rebellion of 1554 30, 88,
    95, 106

Y

York, House of 6, 11–12, 16–18,
    72–73
Younger, Neil 116–117

First published in 2017 by
Connell Guides
Spye Arch House
Spye Park
Lacock
Wiltshire
SN15 2PR

10 9 8 7 6 5 4 3 2 1

Copyright © Connell Guides Publishing Ltd.
All rights reserved. No part of this publication
may be reproduced, stored in a retrieval system or transmitted in any
form, or by any means (electronic, mechanical, or otherwise) without
the prior written permission of both the copyright owners
and the publisher.

A CIP catalogue record for this book is available from the British Library.
ISBN 978-1-911187-48-6

Design © Nathan Burton

Assistant Editor:
Paul Woodward

Printed in Great Britain

www.connellguides.com